BESIDE THE BOWERY

Photo by Rogers & Hewing.

THE LADY OF GOOD CHEER

BESIDE THE BOWERY

BY
JOHN HOPKINS DENISON

SOMETIME PASTOR OF THE
CHURCH OF THE SEA AND LAND

NEW YORK
DODD, MEAD & COMPANY
1914

COPYRIGHT, 1914,
BY DODD, MEAD AND COMPANY

CONTENTS

ILLUSTRATIONS

INTRODUCTION

THERE are lives so full of inspiration and self-sacrifice and faith, that one feels the wish to hold fast the memory of every detail, and to place them in some treasure house impregnable to the assaults of time, where each event and word may be preserved. Such a life Eliza Rockwell lived among the folk of many lands and many needs in the crowded tenements beside the Bowery. The story of her life is written so deeply into the lives of many hundreds that it might easily be read by any who would take the pains. But her work was hidden away in the narrow crowded streets under the shadow of Brooklyn Bridge, and there are few of the upper world who know even her name. Those who have known her personality will always treasure every memory of her life and work, and it is chiefly for their sake that the author has collected these memories of her life among the people whom she loved better than her own health and happiness.

Few of her friends will ever forget the service held in her memory in the old Church of the Sea and Land, close to the Bowery, in the neighbourhood where she had worked so long. The church was filled from the pulpit to the doors by men and women whom she had helped in the hour of their sorest need. Their presence was no formal or perfunctory matter. They came, moved by deepest reverence and love, for they knew that she had laid down her life for them. There was scarcely a dry eye in the church as they looked for the last time on her form, worn out by hard and faithful work in their behalf. There was hardly a soul there to whom she had not brought life and hope in some hour of sickness or despair. I looked into one face after another and remembered all the bitter struggles with hunger and disease and sin in which she had borne a part. I pictured each as he had been and saw what through her he had become. I wished that all men might see what I saw, and understand what one brave, self-sacrificing life may do to transform humanity.

An ordinary description of Eliza Rockwell would convey to a stranger not the slightest idea of what she really was. To depict certain persons, it is needful only to tell how they looked; and from the contour of the chin, the flash of the eye, the cut of a gown, one knows them altogether. To reveal others, one must tell what they said, and in the burning torrent of words or the brilliant epigram, the soul of the man is revealed. Still other characters one can make clear only by describing what has happened to them, and we discover the shape of their souls by examining the world of environing circumstance which has formed them. There are a few, however — and these perhaps are the greatest souls — of whom but little may be learned by these methods. To know them, we must look not at their faces, but at the faces of those about them; we must note not their words, but the deeds of those to whom they have spoken; we must examine not the mould in which the world has shaped them, but the impress which their lives have set upon the world. As they pass, like some hidden magnet, they transform the relations of all things about them. For in them, concealed beneath an unpretending exterior and commonplace words and everyday events, lies the great force that casts down the mighty from their seats, and lifts up the poor out of the dunghill.

Such a character was that of Eliza Rockwell.

It is, therefore, not the purpose of this book to present the reader with an ordinary biography of personal description and facts in chronological order. It is enough to condense such a biography into briefest outline. Mrs. Rockwell lived the earlier part of her life in Binghamton, N. Y. After the death of her husband, she came to New York to study in the Training School for Christian Workers of the New York City Missions. She started on her work at the Church of the Sea and Land in 1894, and continued there for fifteen years. For those who did not know her, we might add that she was tall and slender almost to frailty;

her face somewhat long in contour, with strong, firm chin and high forehead and aquiline nose; her mouth rather large, with straight determined lips; her eyes deep set and penetrating. But no amount of biographical and descriptive detail would give even the faintest idea of the real woman. It is only as one sees the effect of her life on the men and women with whom she lived that one begins to discern what manner of person she was. Under her influence lives that were cold and hard grew warm and sensitive; wooden insensibility was transformed into living, tender humanity, and brutal cruelty into courtesy; base appetites gave way to visions of the spirit, and despair yielded to hope,— and it is only as one sees her soul so reflected in the lives of others that one begins to understand what she herself was.

It has, therefore, been the aim of the author in the sketches which follow to picture as accurately as possible a few of the men and women whom she knew and loved; because it is in their lives that those who knew her can see her as she truly was; and it is in the mirror of their deeds and lives alone that those who never knew her may hope to find a true image of her spirit.

Those who through these pages may learn to see Eliza Rockwell as she was, cannot fail in some measure to share her interest in the men and women to whom she gave her life, different though their circumstances and characteristics may seem from those of that world with which we are familiar. Amid the over-refinements of civilisation and culture we sometimes forget the great mass of men who are struggling fiercely with almost primitive passions, men for whom the A B C of the moral code — the things we take for granted — are a matter of difficult, even of desperate, achievement. In contrast to the subtle analyses of the modern psychological novel, and the hair-splitting ethics of the romanticist, and the exaggerated remorse of the neurasthenic, there is a desperate reality about the battle of this frail woman with the brute passions of men for the great fundamentals of morality, that makes much of our best effort seem in comparison a mere beating of the air.

Those who read stories of the slums to be assured that, frightful though such an environment would be to us, to the poor themselves these conditions afford plentiful amusement and abundant opportunities of happiness, will find little satisfaction in these pages. Nothing can be more untrue to fact, or more immoral in effect than the cheap optimism characteristic of much so-called "Slum Literature," which is really only a sop flung to the consciences of those who, in a city where such conditions exist, enjoy comfortable homes and happy lives without stirring a finger to better those conditions. Literature can only be pernicious in its effect if it leads men to suppose that environment counts for nothing, and that when a man is out of work, half starved, subject to bad habits, and living in the old-time Cherry Street tenement, it requires only a little religion to make him happy and prosperous. A slight acquaintance with the work of Mrs. Rockwell makes one realise that the terrible suffering of the poor in our great cities calls for remedies far more radical than the mere preaching of the gospel of redemption and the expression of personal friendliness. Under such conditions honesty and virtue and happiness are so difficult of attainment as to seem almost miraculous in the case of those who realise them, and the fact that men are willing to struggle toward them against such desperate odds, and that at times they do succeed in attaining them, should give an assurance that when such men receive a fair chance they will respond to it in a way that will abundantly repay the efforts made in their behalf.

It would be difficult to exaggerate the distress and wretchedness of the men and women described in these sketches, for Mrs. Rockwell's work in New York covered those terrible years when thousands of able-bodied workingmen could find no employment, and little children were sent to school day after day with no food. It is not surprising, therefore, that in many cases even one with such extraordinary power over men as she possessed, should have failed; but it should be evident from the narratives that follow that her failures were due to conditions the existence of which is a blot upon a Christian civilisation.

These sketches make no pretence of being well-rounded stories. They are descriptions of actual events and of real persons, presented as accurately as memory can depict them, in the hope that they may aid in preserving to those who loved her, the thought of one who was possessed of the unfaltering faith that there is no life so perverted but that with a true friend and a fair chance it may be transformed to a thing of worth — one who in that faith gave herself and all that she had to the service of her neighbours beside the Bowery.

I

INGENUITY ASKEW

THERE is a certain fascination about canvassing the ancient tumble-down tenements of lower New York. Each door opens upon some new and strange type of life. One sees side by side the flags of all nations, and reads inscriptions in every language from Hebrew and Greek to Chinese. One passes at a step from Syria to Lithuania, from Sicily to furthest Russia and Japan. One may enter upon a mixed-ale party or a rag-pickers' bee, a sweat-shop or a dive. One meets every sort of greeting, from the whining welcome of the beggar to the resentful curse of an anarchist.

Of all the homes into which the Lady of Good Cheer entered on her journeys of friendship the one which impressed her perhaps most vividly with its strangeness was one which she discovered on a winter day in a wretched old tenement in Water Street. It was a season when thousands were out of work and the distress was so great that she had been asked to go through the poorest tenements in search of those who were actually starving and who had not found the city's sources of relief. As she ascended from door to door, she was greeted by responses in almost every known tongue, and when she reached the fourth floor of the tenement and knocked at one of the doors, it was a pleasant surprise to hear a "Come in," in good broad Scotch.

The Lady of Good Cheer was by no means prepared, however, for the scene which met her eyes as she entered the room. Its chaotic contents made it appear like the headquarters of some queer Demiurge who was attempting to equip a world with some new and strange form of vegetation. The floor was piled high with dry stalks, and brown bushes, and withered weeds, and shrubs; and beside them were heaps of some kind of vegetable matter of an unnaturally vivid shade of green. Nearby she was horrified to see a huge tub filled with blood or something that counterfeited it successfully. A neighbouring vat contained a bright green poisonous-looking liquid. Over it bent a wiry little Scotchman with dark side whiskers, a sharp nose, a sharp chin and sharper eyes. His face was decorated with a colour scheme which rivalled that of an Indian brave. Green was the predominant shade, but the weird and ghastly appearance which it imparted was fortunately relieved by a few brilliant dashes of scarlet and gold. Opposite this chromo sat a woman with a good homely Scotch face and keen brown eyes, one of which persisted in a special independent twinkle of its own, while the other glowered in a questioning scowl. She was busily engaged in tying up bundles of flowers, whose odd shape and vivid hues would have given Linnæus a troubled half-hour before he could have discovered a Latin phrase sufficiently profane to do them justice. There was a singular and penetrating odour about the whole place, an odour at once pungent and yet suggestive of some heavy and overpowering perfume. The room seemed full of children. Two little girls were helping their mother gather and bind the stalks. A small boy also lent occasional aid, while a smaller child played on the floor. A baby was asleep on the bed, the only article of furniture in the room which was not piled high with the materials of their labour.

The Scotchman turned his decorated countenance slightly toward the Lady of Good Cheer. The sharp nose, standing out like an illuminated capital in scarlet and gold, added emphasis to the snappy query: "Who are you?"

She explained herself as best as she could, but not to his satisfaction.

"Well, if ye come frae a kirk ye can get out o' here!" he said. "They're all fakes, frauds and liars! I know 'em and I want none of 'em!"

"Don't talk like that, Tom," said his wife. "I know her. She's a good lady and she's helped lots o' poor folks around here. Don't mind him," she said to the Lady of Good Cheer, "he's terrible cranky about the church. Some of the church people treated him awful mean, an' he'll never forgive 'em."

The Lady of Good Cheer sat on the edge of a chair full of bushes, patted the head of a little girl who stood by, and talked with the mother, while the man worked on in sulky silence.

The man did his best to freeze out the Lady of Good Cheer, but something in her voice as she chatted, seemed gradually to wake old associations in his mind, and he listened in spite of himself. Her voice had the singular power of suggesting even to the most unimpressionable some softening memory of a mother or of a home. It struck the note of the eternal womanliness! He looked up at some casual appeal, and caught the twinkle in her kindly eyes, that were surveying him as one might look at an absurdly petulant child. Her firm lips and strong chin were quite as determined as his own square Scotch jaw, and somehow, before he knew it, he had capitulated, and was talking as if he had known her all his life.

He recounted to her, how, in desperation because he was out of work, he had devised this extraordinary employment. Over in the Jersey flats he had found growing a weed with a tall stalk and prickly pod, which opened into a sort of star. He gilded the centres of these and painted the prickly calyx a bright scarlet. Then he gathered a mass of brown vegetation which he dyed bright green and tied up in bunches with the scarlet and gold flowers. Being a good salesman he had succeeded in leaving a couple of these bunches in exchange for a quarter in nearly every tenement, advocating them as an incomparable ornament for the mantelpiece. The people of the tenements were unable to resist the charms of these gorgeous blooms, which were guaranteed never to wither, and he prospered greatly.

There was also a subordinate source of revenue. He had discovered a spot where skunk cabbage grew in profusion. He thought the plants interesting and unusual, and dug them up and brought them home, but the unpleasant odour reduced their market value to zero. He had accordingly hit on the idea of pouring citronella perfume into the cup of the plant. It retained the perfume, which combined with its original odour to make something quite new and entirely unrecognisable in the olfactory sphere. Then he potted the plants and sold them as "Japanese lilies." The East Side not being skilled in botanical analysis was charmed by these strange oriental flowers, and delighted with their rare perfume, and bought all he could prepare. He calculated to adopt another business before the citronella wore off and left the original nauseating odour.

The Lady of Good Cheer entirely won the Donald family, and they became loyal attendants at church. For a year or so everything prospered. They were very religious, they knew the Bible thoroughly, and were to all appearances honest, and earnest in prayer. Then something began to go wrong. They ceased to prosper. Donald had at length glutted the market for scarlet and gold bouquets, and Japanese lilies were no longer in good odour with the public. He had found other employment, but lost it without adequate cause. Things went from bad to worse. One day the Lady of Good Cheer found little Agnes barefoot and ragged, begging in the street. She went to hunt up the family and found the mother and six children,— a new baby had just arrived,— huddled in a wretched little attic in Cherry Street, and there enshrined in the place of honour upon the kitchen table was the dark squat Divinity to whose malevolent influence she at once ascribed the change in their fortune. It needed no further proof that they had betaken themselves to the worship of evil spirits, when there before her stood the visible evidence thereof — a black bottle.

It was a hard blow to the Lady of Good Cheer. She hated to think that all their earnestness in religion had been a cloak of deception to disguise such a worship as this. It was no trifling matter to her. She gave to the men and women whom she found battling with evil and poverty that passion of love which is itself a Divine gift, and it cut her to the heart to find that she had been deceived. It was this love, disappointed and yet still trusting, that spoke in the burning words with which she reproved the woman before her. Mrs. Donald listened, at first with flushed cheeks and angry eyes, and then with bowed head and hot tears as she recognised the supreme authority that alone has the right to reprove another and enter into the inmost recesses of his soul. Hard though she was, she melted before it into confession. They had both been drinking, and Donald had behaved like a demon. Her face and breast were scarred with his blows. He had driven the children into the street to beg, and had taken for drink the money they brought back. For some days they had lived in sodden intoxication, leaving the children to run wild after each had done his turn at begging.

The Lady of Good Cheer did her utmost to bring Donald to his senses, but he was too far gone in drink to be susceptible to reason or affection. He continued to beat his wife and the children and to drive them out upon the streets to beg. At last the family had to be given up in order to save the children. The Society for the Prevention of Cruelty to Children was called in. Donald was intoxicated and resisted when the agents came; and as a result he was given two months on the Island. Two of the girls and the boy were put in the Juvenile Asylum. The oldest sister and the babies were left with the mother.

When the two months were up, Donald returned sober and penitent, and manifested a great desire to get back his children. The Lady of Good Cheer told him that the Society refused to give them up until he had a decent home for them, and could give good evidence that he was sincere in his renunciation of whiskey. In a year or so, with his wife's help, he had acquired a nice little home. But just as the Lady of Good Cheer began to feel safe about helping him in securing the return of the children, she found evidence that he was drinking again. The more she learned of his former abuse of the children the more she hesitated to put them again into his hands. When she refused her aid, Donald stormed and raged. He denounced her and the church as kidnappers, frauds, and liars. He secured a lawyer who made appeals in behalf of a "poor but honest labourer, robbed of his children by the malice and slander of the church and by the injustice and barbarity of the Gerry Society."

Donald's plea found supporters, as such pleas against the church often do, but it was not until the younger girls were fifteen and sixteen that the father got possession of them again. The Lady of Good Cheer continued to treat him with kindness, and even helped him in one crisis by paying his rent when he was about to be dispossessed. In return, supported by his lawyer, he lost no opportunity to insult her, and to denounce the church. It would have been hard to predict anything but a disastrous future for the reunited family.

One morning the Lady of Good Cheer discovered it plainly written in the pages of *The Sun.* She could not help smiling as she read, at the characteristic cleverness of the daughters of the canny Scot who once supplied the tenements with flowers surpassing all the efforts of Nature; but she felt defeated and depressed to know that all her work had not availed to prevent such extraordinary ingenuity from going wrong. The papers gave an account of the arrest of the girls for obtaining money under false pretences. They pretended to be the daughters of a gentleman of social prominence who had forsaken the elegant leisure of their palatial home on Madison Avenue to go about soliciting funds for a mission in the slums in which their father was interested. They were trained as beggars from the cradle, and now that they were dressed in the becoming gowns bequeathed them by a lady of fashion, they had sufficient beauty and charm to win even greater success than when they were clothed in rags. After they had collected a goodly sum their contributors began to make requests to visit the mission. This was confusing, and threatened to interrupt the income which was flowing in upon them in such rich streams. They were clever enough, however, to expand their scheme to meet the demands. One day after a particularly insistent inquiry from a wealthy contributor, Alice came forward with a suggestion: "I have it, Agnes!" she cried. "We must really have a mission to show these guys. They won't take any more of our dope without."

"What do you mean?" asked Agnes.

"I mean we can rent a hall in the slums, and there are always lots of fool mission workers crazy to hear themselves speak, and we can get some one of 'em to come each night. You can play the piano, and I can do a bit of exhorting if we're up against it for talk. We've got plenty of money to rent a cheap stove and some chairs and a piano, and when we can really show the place, we'll raise twice as much. Only we must have it somewhere where there'll be plenty of ragged old loafers looking for shelter and a chance to sit down."

They worked out the plan to the letter. They selected a favourable spot in Brooklyn, rented a stove, a piano and some chairs and soon had persuaded a goodly number of mission workers to come and help on certain nights. The mission soon was filled with the usual crowd of the destitute, and they were able to tabulate a sufficient number of conversions to increase their income by a considerable amount. In the meantime they had found it expedient to separate from their father and mother, who claimed the lion's share of their funds and spent it on drink. Their parents bitterly resented this desertion, and sought them everywhere, but could find no trace of them.

One night the mother, dispossessed of her home

and just recovering from a prolonged spree, saw the open door of the mission, and tired of walking the streets with her latest babe in her arms, went in to rest. To her utter amazement she beheld her two daughters on the platform. She arose to her feet and prepared to denounce them. Alice saw her standing there, ragged, dishevelled, her hair falling about her ears, and her dirty shawl wrapped around the baby. It was easy to guess her mother's intent to expose them.

She whispered to Agnes: "Look! There's Mother! If she speaks she'll give the whole show away."

She stepped down swiftly to the woman's side and whispered, "If you say a word we're all done for; keep your mouth shut and we'll give you all you want."

Then she returned to the platform and said: "That poor woman has been walking the streets all day with her baby, with nothing to eat. She has no home, no place to sleep, and not a penny in the world. We can't turn her out in the cold with that child. Christ said to take in the strangers, and I am going to take her into my own house. She shall sleep in my own bed, and so long as there is a roof over my head she shall be cared for."

The audience was greatly impressed by her self-sacrificing charity. Some one proposed a collection, and the girls soon had in their possession a considerable sum of money, which they devoted to fitting out their mother with more suitable garments.

For a time their colossal deceit worked smoothly, but the father was on their trail. He tracked his wife, and when he found her, there was such a violent altercation that the neighbours sent for the police. The case was thoroughly investigated by the Associated Charities and the girls were arrested.

Alice and Agnes were highly indignant at this turn of affairs. "Why should we be arrested?" they said. "We work for a living. If any one thinks it's a soft snap to run a mission every night in the year, and raise money for it every day, let him try it. They say we spend some of the money given for the mission on ourselves to go to the theatre and all that, but so does this agent of the Charities that hasn't been arrested. Where does he get the money he spends from his salary to go to the theatre? Some one gave it to the Charity Society for their work with the poor. A person must have a little fun now and then." The Court did not respect their indignation nor appreciate their arguments. They had at last reached a place where they could no more be helped by the love and patience of the friend whom they had rejected, and it was the hand of the law which at length dealt the Donald family its "*coup de grace*."

II

A LIVING WAGE

THE Lady of Good Cheer was devoted to all the dwellers in her district, but like all of us she had her favourites, and one of these was old Mrs. Larkins. There were those for whom the dirty crowded tenements of Cherry Hill seemed a natural habitat. They had found their own place, in obedience to the resistless law of gravitation, and she appreciated that if she removed them to higher spheres, they would only sink again to the same dead level, unless first she could put into them a new spirit. When this was accomplished, she found that they rose spontaneously into a better environment. There were others, however, who did not belong in Cherry Street, and who were held down by the operation of laws which she felt increasingly to be unjust and inhuman. Though in most cases, salvation depended on a change in the individual,— in cases such as these it seemed to involve a change in the whole social and industrial order.

She felt this especially when she looked at Mrs. Larkins, and saw the clear-cut, regular features, the high brow and the smooth, evenly-parted, white hair, the cheeks thin and pale from lack of food, but still fair and unfurrowed by wrinkles, and then noted the quaint old bonnet, the pathetic, worn coat and the skirt,— clean but patched in a score of places. Every line and stitch in the clothing told the story of cruel want and desperate need, just as every line in the face spoke of a character faithful to all virtue, an intelligent mind and a brave spirit.

News had reached the Lady of Good Cheer that Mr. Larkins, who had long been ill and out of work, was very sick, and she at once determined to call. She made her way with some difficulty up a black stairway in an ancient dwelling house in Catherine Street. When she had reached what seemed to be the top, she turned to one side and groped her way to the winding stairs that led yet nearer to the sky. She knocked on the door at the top, and entered a true attic room. Here there seemed to be hardly a square yard of wall or ceiling that was not interrupted by some queer angle. The roof was high enough to accommodate a giant on one side, and on the other even a Tom Thumb would have felt obliged to stoop. The only light came through a dormer window which interrupted the slope of the ceiling, and which was set so high that a Goliath could not have looked through it. On a bed at one side lay a man. His head was the head of a philosopher, with a high, bulging forehead seamed with wrinkles. His hair and close-cropped moustache were grey. His clear-cut, aquiline nose and keen, dark eyes that looked out beneath bushy brows betokened intellectual force of a type that is not accustomed to make its habitat in a fourth-ward attic.

At a table near by Mrs. Larkins sat sewing. A large pile of trousers lay beside her on the table. She had a pair in her hands, and was sewing with feverish haste, holding her work close to her spectacled eyes. She did not even stop working when the Lady of Good Cheer entered.

"How do you do!" said Mrs. Larkins. "I'm glad to see you. It's the lady from the church," she added with a glance at the sick man.

He responded by a grunt, which could hardly have been interpreted as an enthusiastic welcome.

"Excuse me if I keep on working," the woman continued. "I've got to finish these trousers to-day somehow. How I'm going to do it, I'm sure I don't know," and she glanced at the huge pile with a long-drawn sigh.

"Certainly, go right on with your work," said the Lady of Good Cheer. "I heard Mr. Larkins was sick, and came in to see if there was anything I could do."

"If you came in to read the Bible or the Prayer Book to me, you may just as well go away," said the old man crustily. "I've been a printer for nearly fifty years, and I've set up enough stuff about the Bible to know there isn't any truth in it;

and as for a God, you won't find many printers who believe in any such thing. You can fool these ignorant people around here all you want, but a printer has to keep up with the thought of the world. He doesn't take any stock in your old superstitions. I've set up plenty of articles in my time that proved as plain as could be that there wasn't any God."

This tirade did not rouse the Lady of Good Cheer to antagonism. She was looking at him closely, trying to determine whether this was merely a pose, or whether his words were sincere.

"But don't you sometimes wish that you had God's help?" she said at last.

"Nonsense! What do I want God's help for?" he answered testily. "I can do what's right if I want to,— if there is such a thing as right and wrong."

"I think most of us find it very hard always to do what is wisest and best," said the Lady of Good Cheer. "We find that we do foolish things in spite of ourselves, and then have to suffer for them."

"That's true enough," broke in the woman. "What's the use of talking, John? You know you wouldn't have lost your job and got sick if you hadn't been terrible foolish."

"I've never harmed any man," said the man, "and if a man wants to drink a glass now and then there isn't anything wrong in that. He's got a right to do as he chooses with his life."

"Do you feel satisfied with what you've done with your life?" asked the Lady of Good Cheer.

The old man remained silent a moment. The keen grey eyes wandered from her face, and seemed to be looking far away into the past. "I'm not saying I didn't hope for something different," he said at last. "We were born on the old island of Jersey in the Channel, and when we got married and started to come over here we thought we were going to do great things, didn't we?" he went on. "I never thought to be lying in a great garret with nothing to eat and my wife working herself to death to keep a roof over our heads. It's shameful the way they pay a woman for working," he added with a sudden flash in the keen eyes. "It's all wrong. If there was a God, he would straighten out some of these things, I can tell you. I'm not any too good myself, but if I was God I wouldn't let them grind down wretched women with hard work and starve them with poor pay in any world I made. How much do you think they give her for finishing those trousers?"

"I don't know," said the Lady of Good Cheer. "Perhaps as little as ten cents apiece."

"Ten cents apiece! They give her eighteen cents a dozen pair, and work as hard as she can, she can't do more than a dozen a day. Our rent is little enough here, but she can't even pay that, let alone buying food. Do you think a just God would stand a world like that?"

"It is terrible," said the Lady of Good Cheer, "too terrible for words. But they say that the kind of work which is done by women at home wouldn't be done at all unless it could be done so cheaply. It does seem as if they ought to pay more, or else that the work ought not to be done. I've just been to see some people in Cherry Street. The man is out of work and has two little children. His wife found a chance to make those little round boxes that they use for charlotte russe. I went in and found them working like mad creatures, while the children played on the floor near by. The woman was pasting, the man fitting the cardboard together and piling up the boxes. How much do you think they got for making those boxes? They got $1.80 for 5,000! They could just clear their rent and get a bit to eat by working furiously from dawn into the night. I know another girl whose father and mother are both crippled. She tries to support the family by making artificial flowers. She does best with violets and they give her twenty-five cents a gross,— a quarter for making 144 flowers!"

"It's not right, I tell you," said the old printer. "As long as any human being is giving his best skill and strength to his work, he ought to get enough to pay to keep him,— yes, and enough so that he could have a little fun out of life; and I tell you if any just God had the ordering of this world he'd see that it was arranged that way."

"Perhaps he is arranging it," the Lady of Good Cheer said. "If we were all true Christians things would be about as you want them, wouldn't they?"

"Perhaps they would," he asserted, "but that won't happen this year."

"We can each one of us start in and do our best," she replied. "That will be a beginning at least."

"It won't do any good for me to start," he said. "When you've made good Christians out of all the rich men and employers, come to me and perhaps I'll join in."

III

THE ECONOMIC VALUE OF A HUSBAND

"It's a comfort to make a call once in a while on a good normal, respectable working family," thought the Lady of Good Cheer, as she started to climb the steps of a neatly kept, old-fashioned house in Cherry Street. One gets tired of finding a skeleton in every house, especially among the poor, who have no closets in which to conceal it, and the Lady of Good Cheer felt the need of a commonplace conversation about housekeeping and dressmaking and babies and other normal subjects of feminine interest. Mrs. Finley's house was in pleasing contrast with the squalid and poverty-stricken home she had been visiting. There was a well-furnished parlour into which Mrs. Finley ushered her distinguished visitors, throwing open the blinds to illuminate the gaily coloured chromos on the walls, and the satin scarfs that decked the mantel and adorned the back of the plush sofa.

Mrs. Finley was always saluted by that name, in spite of the fact that she was married to Mr. Hart. Perhaps the old name persisted because Miss Rose Finley, her daughter by her former marriage, focussed the attention of the public. Miss Rose was a very pretty girl of sixteen with a fluffy mass of golden hair, a pink and white complexion, and red and pouting lips. Her name was familiar through that block in Cherry Street, and was naturally transferred to her mother. Moreover, Mr. Hart was an insignificant-looking, elderly workingman, wizened and wiry, who never seemed to have anything to say for himself, but went to his work regularly every morning, and did not return until nightfall.

The Lady of Good Cheer looked at her watch as she knocked at the door, allowing herself ten minutes of quiet conversation with Mrs. Finley before she returned to her problems. It was a somewhat broken voice that called "Come in," and she entered to find Mrs. Finley sitting with her apron to her eyes, sobbing distressfully.

"Oh, Mrs. Finley! What is it?" she asked. "Has anything happened?"

"I can't stand it no longer," sobbed Mrs. Finley. "It ain't no use tryin'. There ain't nobody as has such troubles as me, and I'm just clean beat out."

The Lady of Good Cheer sought to mask her amazement. So there was a skeleton here, of all places! She would sooner have looked for one in a butler's pantry! What could it be? Her thoughts went at once to the daughter. She must be the cause of the trouble.

"Has anything happened to Rose?" she asked. "Do tell me if I can do anything to help."

"Oh, it's too awful!" Mrs. Finley sobbed. "To think that my daughter should ever hear such things and see such things! If she isn't ruined it will be a wonder."

The Lady of Good Cheer was more and more mystified. To construct a skeleton out of such very commonplace family materials was a task for the imagination that was beyond her. She could only sit and wait till the closet door was opened.

"It wasn't like this when Mr. Finley was alive," the woman went on. "He was a decent hard-working man, and he always treated me like a lady."

Then the skeleton had its hiding-place in Mr. Hart's coat tails. So much was evident. But what mysterious diabolism could work under the form of that wizened old workingman?

"Has Mr. Hart done anything wrong to you?" she asked.

Mrs. Finley, ordinarily a quiet, self-contained, woman, was utterly beside herself to-day. Her suffering had reached a point where it must find expression.

"Oh, he's a terrible man!" she burst forth. "You wouldn't believe it to look at him, but he's near killed me again and again. Last night he beat me within an inch o' me life. An' I had the house all fixed up for him and a nice supper on the table. But he was that cranky that nothing suited him, and he cursed me and threw the dishes on the floor. Such language! It ain't fit for my daughter to hear such talk. He comes home drunk every Saturday night, and he's as cross as a bear. You can't get a word out o' him that isn't a curse. He'll be the death o' me — I tell you I can't stand it no longer. Me an' him has got to part."

"I don't blame you for feeling as you do," said the Lady of Good Cheer, who had listened in amazement at this unexpected outburst. "No one believes more than I do in a wife's standing by her husband, but you have your daughter to think of, and this man is not the father of your children. If he is what you say he is, and nothing will make him treat you decently, I think you are perfectly right in separating from him. You can come up to the church on Thursday night and see the lawyer there and he will draw up the papers for you."

Mrs. Finley took her apron from her eyes and stopped sobbing. "You mean for me to get a separation from me husband?" she asked.

"Yes," said the Lady of Good Cheer. "I'll help you if you wish. It is terrible that you should be treated so."

"Yes, it's mighty bad," said Mrs. Finley, slowly drumming on the table with her fingers, "but you see, I don't know as I'd best get a *separation.*"

"You mean you'd rather have a divorce?

That would be much more difficult. I don't know if that could be done."

"No, I don't believe I want a divorce."

"Well, what do you want? If you are to be protected from this man, you must have a separation or a divorce."

"Well, I don't know. Maybe I was too hasty. It does seem terrible hard, but I don't believe I want a separation."

"What! Do you really care for him in spite of all?"

"Care for him!" said Mrs. Finley. "Yes, I love him just like I would the grizzly bear in the zoo if he was me husband. Bah! I hate the sight of him."

"Well, then, why don't you want a separation?"

"Well, you see some ways he treats me pretty good, better'n lots o' husbands I know. He always brings his money home regular every Saturday. He keeps two dollars for the drink and hands over ten dollars to me. 'Tain't every wife as gets the whole o' ten dollars when her man's only making twelve."

"That is a good point, certainly," said the Lady of Good Cheer. "It seems to show that he cares more for you than many men do for their wives."

"Cares for me! Not much he doesn't! He treats me like dirt."

"But I don't understand. Why don't you want to leave him?"

"Well, you see, after Mr. Finley died I had a terrible hard time. I had to scrub and wash, and, work as hard as I could, we pretty near starved to death. Now I get ten dollars a week, and that's enough to keep up a nice home. There ain't many men would give me that much, neither. Of course it's hard,— his beatin' and cursin' me every Saturday and Sunday when he's home; but it ain't nowhere near so hard as workin' all week till your back's broke, and you can't see straight, and all your body hurts like you'd been pounded, fer a promise of five dollars, and never knowin' when you'll get kicked out to starve. You see it's like this: Husbands is mighty mean to live with, but you can't live at all without 'em. It's a sight better to have a nice home, and put up with a row oncet a week, than to live a dog's life all the time. When a woman's married she's only got one man to knock her around a bit now and then, but when she's alone, every one's knockin' her around all the time, and she never knows when she'll be turned onto the street to die o' starvation. I guess I know. I ain't lived that way five years for nothin'. I get discontented-like now and then, but in me heart I know what's good for me. When I've got a husband I know enough to stick to him."

IV

A TWIG TRANSPLANTED

"If I get enough money to move you to another house, will you try to keep it clean and get rid of these old rags?" asked the Lady of Good Cheer of Mrs. Malloy.

She was standing in a dark basement room, for she did not dare to sit down. The room was littered with great piles of dirty rags and broken implements that were heaped everywhere against the wall, under the table and in the chairs. There were black rags, blue rags, red rags, and above all brown rags once white. It looked as if the woman had picked up every filthy scrap from the tenement yards and stored it, as the bibliophile litters his room with choice and ancient editions. The odour of this soiled decaying mass of rags was so unspeakably offensive that the Lady of Good Cheer felt positively ill. The thought that a man and his wife and two children actually lived in this refuse heap, filled her with disgust and horror. She would have preferred to sleep on an ash heap in the open air rather than be shut up in a dark basement with this hoard of garbage. The woman was not an Italian ragpicker. The Lady of Good Cheer knew many such in Cherry Street whose rooms were piled high with carefully assorted bales of rags. There was no reason for this insane collection of dirty poisonous refuse, other than some queer quirk in the woman's mind which led her to cling to every soiled scrap that came within her reach.

Again and again the Lady of Good Cheer had begged Mrs. Malloy to clean house and get rid of this mass of debris for the children's sake. Several times the woman had promised to destroy her strange collection, but it seemed that she really could not nerve herself to make the sacrifice. She was a shrunken, apologetic little person, arrayed in a selection of her own rags, so that she looked like a third-class scarecrow,—by no means the distinguished type that wears a complete suit of clothes, and stands erect and defiant with outstretched arms threatening the thief, but the kind that is patched up with all sorts of remnants, and that stands battered and browned by the weather, all huddled and shrunken in the consciousness that all men and birds must be repelled by its grotesque ugliness. Her husband, a stout cumbrous man, with a fat, heavy, and unintelligent face, sat and stared at the Lady of Good Cheer with the blankness of a Chinese idol. His round bulging eyes seemed to gaze through her into vacancy, and it was sometime before she discovered he was almost blind. There was a bright-faced little girl, and a boy full of the quick nervous energy that characterises the New York street urchin. The Lady of Good Cheer was determined that during their years of growth they should not have this rag heap for their only home.

Fortune favoured the Lady of Good Cheer. To-day when she called she learned that the family was to be dispossessed. They were without funds, and desperate, and the visitor saw her opportunity to drive a stern bargain. Mr. Malloy had the chance to take up a business in coal and ice in Hamilton Street, if he could secure the necessary capital.

"If you will let me send little Mamie away to the country, I will try to get enough money to start Mr. Malloy in business," she said.

"Oh, will you?" said Mrs. Malloy, clasping her hands in cringing gratitude. "How can I thank you! If we could only get money to move and get started in business everything would be all right again, wouldn't it, Tim?"

Mr. Malloy made a sound between a growl and a grunt, which might have been expressive of gratitude or resentment. They were both people of some education who had seen better days, but little by little through his blindness and her strange penchant for rags and dirt, they had sunk to the degradation in which the Lady of Good Cheer had found them.

At length the bargain was consummated in spite of the unresponsive grunts of Mr. Malloy.

Mamie, a frail, pale child clothed in the best rags her mother could pick from the heap, was sent to the country. It was a novel enough experience for her, and she looked forward to it with enthusiasm. She had heard of the woods and fields and longed to see their wonders. As she drove away from the country station, the road led between some huge piles of logs corded and ready for shipment. Through her father's trade in combustibles, she was familiar with coal and wood and had naturally thought of the forests as the inexhaustible source of the wood she had seen. In school she had heard much of the woods, and she looked forward to seeing a forest as soon as she reached the country. As they drove between the piles of corded firewood, she cried excitedly: "Are those the woods? Say, are those the woods?" It took the old farmer, who was driving, some time to realise that this child of the city was actually so ignorant of Nature as to suppose that these piles of logs were a primitive forest. She was placed in a nice old farm house, far away from the noise of the railroads and from all association with city life. Here the days went by while she learned to feed the chickens, milk the cow, peel the potatoes and dig in the garden. Slowly she was metamorphosed from the pale, nervous child of the city, to a fat-limbed, rosy-cheeked country girl.

In the meantime the Malloys moved, the necessary capital being duly supplied by the Lady of

Good Cheer. Some days later she called at their new dwelling. She entered a low basement far below the level of the street. The front room was half full of coal, which was strewn all over the floor. The black dust was on the walls and windows, on the chairs and table, on the coat and face of Mr. Malloy, who sat in an armchair, staring with his unblinking goggle eyes, more josslike than ever. The walls were hung with the dirty hats, coats and shovels of the street cleaning department, for Mr. Malloy had cleverly added to his business by making his store a checking office for the garments of the street cleaners, whose station was adjacent. The Lady of Good Cheer passed by the unblinking joss who saluted her with a grunt, and paused in dismay at the door of the room behind. This was the space reserved for family life. It was totally dark. No ray of light entered save from the room in front, but even this feeble illumination sufficed to reveal the piles of dirty rags with which it was strewn. There was not a corner of the stifling narrow room that was not heaped with dirty refuse. In these cramped quarters, the mass of debris looked more appalling than ever.

The Lady of Good Cheer was about to remonstrate over this flagrant breach of contract, when she saw that Mrs. Malloy, seated in the midst of her choice collection, was rocking to and fro and sobbing and moaning. "Oh, what shall I do," she cried again and again. The inquiries of the Lady of Good Cheer finally elicited the information that Willie had been accused of stealing a dollar from the pocket of one of the coats of the Street Cleaning Department that hung in the shop.

"Such a good boy as he is," Mrs. Malloy added indignantly. "As soon as he gets home from school, he takes his papers and off he goes to sell them. Many's the day we'd have had no food but for Willie and his papers. Then he comes home and helps his father with the coats and shovels, when the street cleaners go off duty. You see Mr. Malloy can't see, and what he'd do without Willie I don't know. He has been playing hookey from school lately, I know, and he's got in with some of these bad Hamilton Street boys, but I don't believe my Willie would steal."

Willie was indeed a bright boy, with that astonishingly quick intelligence which is often developed by the rough competition of city life, and the Lady of Good Cheer had hopes that he would distinguish himself some day.

He was always ready for any emergency. If one of the gang had his foot run over, it was Willie who bound up the wounded member with deft fingers and who carried his helpless comrade on his own shoulders to the nearest dispensary.

One evening not long before the boys had been playing basketball in the Hamilton Street Club rooms, when one of them hit the gas jet with the ball and broke it off. The gas poured out in a fountain of flame that licked the ceiling and threatened to destroy the house. There were two young men from up town in charge of the club, but in face of such an emergency, they stood aghast and helpless. They knew no way to quench that roaring fountain of fire that was spouting destruction. Quick as a flash a small urchin darted into a corner, threw open a trap door, dived into it, and gave a quick turn of his wrist. Instantly flame and lights went out, and the room was left in darkness. The club leaders stood utterly amazed, wondering what *deus ex machina* had intervened in so unaccountable a way to save them from so imminent a disaster. It was sometime before they realised that the gas had been shut off where it entered the house. How any small urchin had found out where the gas pipes ran, or discovered the way to turn it off, remained a mystery. And they found it still more amazing that, granted the knowledge of these things, a mere child should have had sufficient self-possession and intelligence to do on the second the one thing that availed to save them from a conflagration, which in that crowded tenement district might have resulted in indescribable horrors.

The boy that shut off the gas was Willie Malloy, and the Lady of Good Cheer felt that he was worth some trouble. She had tried to transplant him along with his sister, for she saw that the en-

Photo by J. H. Denison.

PROMPT AID TO THE INJURED

vironment of Hamilton Street was rapidly transforming him. His father would not listen to the proposition. They needed Willie "in their business."

The Lady of Good Cheer relieved Mrs. Malloy's distress by promising to do everything in her power to save him from the consequences of his misstep. On the day of the trial, she went to plead his case in court. As it was a first offence, he was let off on probation. But the poisonous soil of Hamilton Street was too powerful an element to be counteracted by the advice of a probation officer. It was to her like living in the very shadow of death.

In spite of the most strenuous efforts of the Lady of Good Cheer reinforced by the truant officer, Willie could not be kept in school for more than two consecutive days. There was always some excuse forth-coming, and it soon became evident that his delinquency was by orders of his father who found Willie's financial abilities of increasing value in his complicated business. Though utterly impervious to the mathematics of the school, he acquired with astonishing facility the less legitimate methods of addition and subtraction in vogue in Hamilton Street, and while the ethical and political ideals inculcated by the School Reader bored him to exasperation, he was rapidly realising the heroic ideals of the street gang. His boyish countenance was acquiring the hard lines and the look of brutal cynicism which characterises the portraits of those distinguished personages whose likenesses are preserved in that gallery which his comrades regarded as the true Hall of Fame,— the archives of the Police Department.

To the Lady of Good Cheer and the Probation Officer he always protested his virtue and diligence with such vividness of language and abundance of circumstantial detail that she could not bring herself to realise the swiftness of his moral descent till she discovered him one day in a dark courtyard at the back door of a saloon, drinking mixed ale out of an ancient and dirty can with a gang of the roughest and toughest little specimens of humanity she had ever seen. This group of small urchins carousing in secret, presented such a hideous travesty on the vices of their elders, that it was long before she recovered from the horror of it.

In the meantime Mamie remained in the farmhouse, far from the attractions of Cherry Hill. She continued to milk the cows, feed the pigs, gather eggs and dig in the garden. Every Sunday she drove to church some three miles away and stayed to Sunday-School. The good mistress of the farm treated her like a daughter, for though she loved children, she had none of her own. No one who saw her would have taken Mamie for a child of the city. In her neat dress and white apron, with her smooth braided hair, and rosy, freckled face, and fat legs and arms she looked like a true farmer's daughter. She spoke no more with the accent of the East Side. She had caught the true Yankee twang and drawl. Everytime the Lady of Good Cheer visited the country she rejoiced in her achievement. Such an arrangement, she felt, was almost too good to be true.

The years passed and the Lady of Good Cheer was becoming assured that one child at least had been permanently saved from the influence of Hamilton Street, when one day the parents met her with a demand for the return of their daughter. "They needed her help," they said. The Lady of Good Cheer thought with horror of her reëntrance into the life of Hamilton Street and into that coal hole which they called home. She talked with the agitated scarecrow and the resentful grunting Joss, day after day, and at last effected a compromise. Mamie should come and visit her father and mother, but it was to be left to her to decide whether she would remain or not. So the eventful day arrived when a fat freckled country maid was taken up to the city. It was now as unknown and exciting a land to her as the country had been five years before when she had mistaken the corded woodpile for a forest. The rush and bustle made her tremble. The hurdy-gurdies and moving picture shows and gaudy theatre posters made her thrill with excitement. The ride in the elevated train was one long marvel.

Then came the walk through the crowded down town streets,— packed with aged Jews and screaming children, and by the time she came to the low basement door, she was quite bewildered. She went down the stairs into the black coal hole and saw the Joss seated in the midst of his array of dirty coats and hats, and staring with unblinking goggle eyes. She went into the dark back room with its foul heaps of rags, and the thin, wizened woman in her scarecrow garments seized her and embraced her. She was filled with fear and disgust and began to cry. This black malodorous cellar did not seem like home, nor these strange rag-clad creatures like a father and mother. She wanted to get away,— never to see them again. But she did not want to leave the city. She wanted to hear its music, to see its pictures, to visit its theatres, to share in its throbbing life again. She did not recognise the ragged lad with his thin pinched face when he came forward to greet her. Indeed, to look at them as they stood side by side, no one would have imagined that they came of the same flesh and blood or even of the same race,— the plump, rosy, freckled girl with her neat dress and slow drawl, and the sharp-faced boy, whose soiled clothes seemed falling to pieces, and who spoke the quick pungent slang of the East Side.

It was an anxious day for the Lady of Good Cheer. She said all she could to prove to Mamie the superiority of country life, and then she had to wait while the crowding impressions of the strange new life made their appeal to the girl. Perhaps if her parents had pressed her less eagerly, she might have stayed. But after the cleanliness of the country, the embraces of the ragged woman in the dirty cellar were too much for her. Education at length triumphed over heredity when the country-girl in Mamie decided against the coal-hole. It was not until she was safe on the train that was to bear her back to the little country village which was henceforth to be her home, that the Lady of Good Cheer felt the strain of anxiety relax, and breathed a sigh of relief. She went home with the image of the two children still in her mind, and she thought to herself, "Two twigs, taken from the same tree! If only the world could see and understand what can be done by transplanting and a little bending."

V

A SONG OF EXORCISM

THE minister was just starting uptown to attend an important function. He had laid aside his usual uniform of rusty clericals, and, arrayed in frock coat and silk hat, and with gloves and silver-headed stick in hand, he presented so unaccustomed a figure of elegance as to elicit a prolonged stare from such members of the Men's Club as were haunting the church house steps, while O'Brien whispered stertorously to Rosenberg: "Say, de boss is off on a spree for sure, dis time!"

The minister was accompanied by a friend from uptown and was in a hurry, but as he passed through the hall the nurse called to him. "Won't you come here a minute and get Mr. Halloran to take this medicine?"

She was engaged in the difficult task of sobering off Mr. Halloran, a gallant ex-member of the King's Hussars. He was a most courtly person when sober, but that morning, being under spirituous influence, he had had an altercation with his wife which had ended in his chasing her from the house axe in hand, while he threatened her in language which would have terrified a cohort of Zulus. It was deemed unsafe to permit him to return home until the effect of the alcohol he had imbibed had been completely counteracted by suitable medicaments.

As the minister stopped, the nurse said to Halloran, " You'll take it if the minister gives it to you, won't you, Mr. Halloran? "

" Sure, I'll do anything fer his Riverence," said Halloran with a genial grin. He was a thin, wiry man with a freckled face, and a large, expressive Irish mouth shaded by a ragged moustache. He walked with the loose-jointed slouch of an ex-cavalryman, but there was a surprising nervous agility about his movements.

As he spoke he rose from his seat behind the table with a sudden jerk, and bowed with exaggerated courtesy. " There's no man in all the world that Oi love as Oi do yer Riverence," he added with another bow.

The minister took the glass and pushed it toward him across the wide table. " There, Halloran, go ahead and take your medicine, that's a good fellow. You know it will do you good."

Halloran reached out for the glass and said, " All right, yer Riverence."

He took the glass in his hand, made a bow to the assembled company, and went on with impassioned volubility: " Why is it that I always does everythin' your Riverence asks me in spite o' meself? Why is it I can't resist the requests ye make o' me? Mr. Rainy asks me to take the medicine and I won't touch it; and Miss Smith asks me to take it, and I leaves it standing there; and the nurse asks me to take it, and I won't do it; — but when your Riverence asks me," and he bowed profoundly, " I takes the glass,"— and he lifted it to his lips, looked at it hard a minute, and concluded, —" an' I sets it down on the table again."

With great solemnity Halloran deposited the glass still unquaffed on the table, while the minister's friend from uptown shouted with laughter, and the nurse and her group of helpers looked grieved and disappointed over their humiliating defeat after an hour of work with the patient.

Just then a little boy rushed in at the door, hatless and breathless. He was a slim, handsome little fellow of about ten, with a clear complexion and regular features, but his face was quite pale, his eyes were terrified, and his hair was flying wildly. He ran to the minister and in an excited whisper, he said: " Me mommer says, ' Come down ter our house quick as yer can! Me popper is drinkin' an' he's took the knife to me mommer and she's afraid he'll kill me little brother an' sister."

" All right," said the minister. " Come along! " and he darted out of the door with the small boy. It was some blocks away and they ran at full speed through the street crowded with Jewish women in shawl and scheitel, with ragged children of all ages and sizes, with pedlars and pushcarts. They turned the corner into Catherine Street, where the sidewalk was filled with throngs of workingmen and shop girls on their way to the ferry. Through the crowd they rushed, — the ragged, bareheaded, barefoot boy and the man in frock coat and top-hat. The crowd stared at them and supposing the small boy to be a pickpocket, pursued by a stray inhabitant of Fifth Avenue, some of the more energetic joined in the chase. By the time they reached the foot of Catherine Street they had aroused quite a commotion in a ward always prone to excitement.

The minister knew there was good cause to hurry. The MacLean family had been given over as a special charge to the church by the Charity Organisation Society. MacLean was a good workman and a man of respectable appearance and very pleasant manners. His wife was an Englishwoman, of quite an unusual type for that neighbourhood, neat in person, a fine housekeeper and a good mother. All would have gone well with them if MacLean had not been possessed of the Scotchman's fondness for his native beverage. Because of that fondness he had lost one position after another, and was now working as longshoreman. When the desire for "Old Scotch" once came upon him, any ordinary dose was only a tantalising irritant.

One day MacLean was assisting in unloading a consignment of whisky from one of the steamers.

The job was about finished, when in some way the Scotchman managed to secure a bottle of the whisky, and drank it almost at one gulp, while the foreman's back was turned. How any one but a professional fire-swallower could stand such a test is a mystery still unsolved. The dose seemed to accelerate the activity of his lanky limbs and to transform him into an animated windmill. He collided joyously and inconsequentially with his fellow workmen, arousing their ire to such an extent that he returned home with a black eye and a broken nose. He demanded money from his wife, and when she refused him, he attempted to take off the children's shoes, a recent gift of the Charity Organisation Society, to carry them to the pawnbrokers. The children wept and resisted, and in sudden rage, he picked up a carving knife from the table and struck at the little girl. His wife caught his arm and screamed. They had a desperate tussle which was fortunately interrupted by the arrival of neighbours. Since then, Mrs. MacLean had lived in constant terror.

MacLean was always full of repentance when he recovered, which did not prevent him from still more devilish behaviour on the next occasion. His digestive system must have been constructed of steel piping, for nothing seemed to put it out of commission. Any ordinary man would have met his death or reached repentance long before.

One morning instead of going to his work, he

made an extensive circuit of the Cherry Street saloons, and discovered an individual whom, in spite of a dilapidated costume and a disfigured countenance, his alcoholic vision recognised as a perfect gentleman and a beloved friend. He returned home with this affectionate companion in quest of further funds. He found his wife absent and some money on the table, and he picked up a pail from the floor and started for the saloon. He should have been sufficiently acquainted with the habits of his tidy housewife to know that she did not leave pails lying about unless they were in immediate use. He was in no mood for psychological inductions, however, and promptly took the pail to the corner saloon and had it filled with beer. When he returned and dipped into the can with his friend, he remarked that the beer had an unusually fine "bead." His friend also noted an especially spicy flavour. The substance sold in the fourth ward under the name of beer or mixed ale is at best a strange compound made up with a basis of high wines and flavoured with various highly astringent chemicals, and though this particular mixture attacked the palate in a fashion which seemed unusual even to MacLean, he only liked it the better, and the pail was soon drained. In a few moments his friend was lying on his back, screaming with agony. The neighbours rushed in, an ambulance was summoned, and he was carried away to the hospital in what seemed his death agony. At last Mrs. MacLean returned. She looked at the pail and at her husband and gave a gasp of horror. As she sank into a chair, she murmured feebly: "I was cleanin' and that pail was a quarter full of lye." MacLean stayed home from work for a day. He informed his anxious friends that the beer had somewhat overstimulated his digestion, but they found his cheerful spirit in no wise disturbed.

These and similar events ran through the minister's mind as he and the urchin raced down the crowded street. Mrs. MacLean had been so certain that the next time her husband drank he would kill her or the children, that the minister had promised to come instantly if she summoned him. Now he was blaming himself for having arranged no more immediate help for her than such as he could give after running five blocks. The poor child with him thought his brother and sister already murdered, and the minister shared his fears. He seemed to see MacLean with his blood-stained knife standing over the bodies of his children — a raging beast whom none could tame. He sprang up the steps of the tenement, two at a time, while the startled inmates stood gaping at this apparent invader from Fifth Avenue, who was so evidently in a hurry to mount their stairs.

The minister was about to throw open the door of MacLean's room when an unexpected sound caught his ear. It was not the curse or groan he had anticipated. It was a man's voice singing in a curious, quavering, unsteady tone. The words and tune sounded strangely familiar. He pushed the door gently open and looked in, and could scarcely restrain a cry of amazement. The man who but a moment before had been an infuriated brute on the verge of murder was kneeling by the sofa. He was dressed in his longshoreman's jumper and ragged trousers, with the leathern belt and iron hook at his waist. His tall, loose-jointed frame sprawled out half on the floor, half on the couch; and at his side knelt the Lady of Good Cheer in her trim suit of dark blue, one slim gloved hand on the back of the sofa and the other resting lightly on his shoulder. Together they were singing, her clear voice rising above his uncertain, quavering bass:

"Just as I am and waiting not
To rid my soul of one dark blot,
To Him whose blood can cleanse each spot,
O Lamb of God, I come, I come."

VI

A TEMPORARY HUSBAND

THE Lady of Good Cheer was seated beside Mrs. Johnson-Schwarz in the well-furnished parlour of a pleasant, four-room apartment. She was attempting to say something that was comforting, for Mrs. Johnson-Schwarz was weeping. She was weeping decorously, however, and at the same time surveying with admiration from the corner of one tearful eye, her new black dress, just purchased at a reduction sale. The Lady of Good Cheer found words difficult, partly because the tragedy was so terrible and partly because Mrs. Johnson-Schwarz seemed to be enjoying her grief in so refined a manner. It seemed almost a sacrilege to attempt to change a mood which was so eminently appropriate to the occasion.

Mrs. Keturah Johnson-Schwarz was a Scotchwoman of medium build with a broad, freckled face, pale blue eyes in which lurked a canny shrewdness, and a mouth whose size and coarseness were forgiven because of its fascinating mobility and variety of expression. Her open countenance had a certain attraction, something of the charm that one finds in the brown face and honest eyes of an intelligent fisher lad. It evidently had a peculiar fascination for men, for she had been several times married. If any one in the ward understood the proper demeanour to observe on the death of a husband she did. Practice had made her perfect.

The Lady of Good Cheer knew little of the antecedents of Mrs. Johnson-Schwarz. She had joined the church and demonstrated that thorough acquaintance with the Scriptures, so characteristic of the Scotch. She was well trained in theology, and was a good critic of sermons. Her two boys, twelve and fourteen years old, bore the name of Johnson, and were the survivals of a former matrimonial dynasty. They had brown complexions and slightly kinky hair, which suggested the theory that the earlier dynasty had been of Nubian origin. On the subject of the character and fate of Mr. Johnson, Mrs. Johnson-Schwarz remained discreetly silent. Mr. Schwarz had been a brutal-faced, low-browed German, in form squat and Simian, and strong as a gorilla. He kept his wife and step-sons in constant terror, but he brought in good wages from his work at unloading the coal steamers, and even after allowing him enough for what he regarded as a satisfactory spree every Saturday night, there was still plenty to provide for a spacious flat and many of the luxuries. Mr. Schwarz hated the church and believed in nothing but dollars and beer.

A few nights before this visit of the Lady of

Good Cheer, Schwarz had gone down to finish unloading a great coal steamer before daybreak. He was standing by the revolving drum on which was wound the chain that hoisted many hundred-weight of coal from the hold below, and was adjusting the chain, when one of the men gave an unexpected signal to start the engine. The drum turned suddenly, catching his hand beneath the chain. Alarmed by his maddened screams, the men at last stopped the engine and reversed it. They picked up a limp mass of flesh and bones, shrieking and cursing like some fiend in torment. They carried him to the hospital and aroused his wife from her sleep. She went to the church and called for the minister, who did what he could to reassure her and to provide for Mr. Schwarz at the hospital. In the morning the Lady of Good Cheer visited him. The man lay on his cot in the hospital with crushed limbs and broken back, groaning, writhing, cursing. He had but a few hours to live, and she was the only one who could prepare this coarse, degraded brute to meet the terrible change which was so close at hand. He met her most sympathetic words with a wolfish snarl, her prayers with a curse; and she left him depressed and disheartened. She found it, therefore, peculiarly hard to speak with his wife of her loss. Besides being incongruous, words of comfort seemed insincere. The Lady of Good Cheer felt that Mrs. Johnson-Schwarz would undoubtedly miss the weekly wage, but not the man who had earned it. She made an end to her call as soon as she could, feeling baffled and incompetent — baffled by the tragedy of a death justly unmourned, and incompetent to criticize an actress so well trained in her part as was Mrs. Johnson-Schwarz.

Some months later the Lady of Good Cheer called upon the widow in the humble quarters into which she had moved after the death of her husband.

"Oh, I'm so glad you've come," said Mrs. Johnson-Schwarz. "I was just coming to the church to ask if you could do anything for this here young man."

She pointed to a man seated in the next room. He was clothed in a loose ragged coat and trousers that seemed ready to disintegrate. He had no shirt or collar. His shoes were worn through and showed more holes and naked feet than leather.

"Come here," she called. "I want to introduce you to this lady. What's your name anyway? I can't remember it."

The man rose, six feet three, vigorous in flesh and blood. Yellow curls clustered around his high white forehead. His features were regular and strikingly handsome, and a small golden moustache curled over his full red lips. He clicked his ragged heels together and bowed profoundly.

"Braunberg-Lichtenstein, bitte," he said. "I speak not very gut English," he added.

"I found him lying in the hallway downstairs last night," said the widow. "He'd crept in out of the rain, and I brought him in and gave him a bed and something to eat, and I thought perhaps you could get some work for him up at the church."

The Lady of Good Cheer looked at him closely. "How did you get into such trouble?" she asked. "You don't look like a tramp or a beggar."

"Ach, madam," he said, "it make me ashame so to speak mit you. Mein Vater ist Prediger — how you say? — preacher? — in Deutschland, und mein Onkel, he has so ein Schloss — a big house — und money, very much money. I vas Offizier in der Deutsche army, but I haf very much money spent. Mein Vater, he vas angry mit mir. He say, 'Go vay. I nefer see you no more.' Now ist mein Onkel dead, und he has much, much money left to me, but I cannot go. I haf no money, no friend."

He spoke with many gestures and a play of expression which was more illuminating than his language. The Lady of Good Cheer asked him to come to the Employment Bureau at the church, and suggested that he consult a lawyer as to securing his property. It was evident that what he said was partly true. He was undoubtedly a young German officer of good social position — every movement of the man verified so much of his story. The true cause of his disgrace, however, might well have been suppressed.

A few weeks later, while the Lady of Good Cheer was busy with her reports at the church, the sexton knocked at the door of her office. In answer to her " Come in! " he said: " Say, that there Mrs. Schwarz, the mother of them two kink-headed kids, you know, is out there, with the swellest young gazabo I ever see in the old fourth ward. He's a peach, a regular fairy, I'm thinkin'."

" Oh, it must be that young German she took in," said the Lady of Good Cheer.

" There's something on the boards fer fair," he went on. " She's rigged up ter kill, and there's a look in her eye,— well, you just take a peep at her yourself," and the sexton rubbed his stubby chin, and his mouth expanded in a reminiscent grin.

Sure enough, there sat Mrs. Johnson-Schwarz in a new dress, black out of deference to the departed, but relieved with many flounces and fugitive dashes of colour. A huge feather on an enormous hat waved over her freckled face. She was blushing coyly, and was studying the floor, save when she cast an occasional swift glance at the man beside her. He was dressed neatly and fashionably, almost as any young German attaché of the legation might be. He wore a well-fitting cutaway coat, and there was a carnation in his buttonhole. His linen was spotless, and his tie, gloves and socks were of harmonious shades. He might easily have been a selfpossessed foreign gentleman of position. The simpering, freckle-faced Scotch working-woman at his side, overwhelmed with the consciousness of her waving plumes and gorgeous apparel, presented a singular contrast.

"Can I speak with you a minute, in private?" she asked.

The Lady of Good Cheer took her into the office and then the widow said: "Me and him's goin' to get married. I s'pose you think it's too soon and all that, but he's been stayin' in my house some weeks now, and the neighbours is beginnin' to talk, and the best we can do is to stop their mouths right away quick."

The Lady of Good Cheer looked at her aghast. She felt that such a match must prove utterly disastrous. At length she managed to say, "But he is so young. Do you think you will get on well together?"

"Oh, I ain't so terrible old as all that," she answered coyly. "And then the boys needs a man in the house to manage 'em. I can't do a thing with 'em, no more."

"But you don't know anything about him," protested the Lady of Good Cheer. "Wouldn't it be wiser to wait until you know if his story is true?"

"Oh, I'm goin' to pay for a lawyer and we're goin' to get that money. It's all true fast enough. I've seen his letters and he's got rich enough relations over there."

Arguments had no effect on the woman. Besides the fact that she was entirely bewitched with the handsome young foreigner, and had spent a good share of her savings in fitting him out, there was a canny Scotch scheme behind the fondness of the amorous widow. She had her eye on the fortune in Germany.

When the minister came down that evening there were several visitors waiting for him. The first was a shy maiden, somewhat advanced in years for the coyness of her demeanour, clad in gay but ill-fitting garments, and wearing a hat surmounted by a scarlet plume.

"I come to see would you marry us," she said, as she cast down her eyes and tried to blush. "Me feller had orter 'ave come but he's a terrible shy feller, so I had ter ax you meself."

"When do you want to be married?" asked the minister.

"To-night at ten o'clock," she answered.

"To-night!" he exclaimed. "That is rushing things too much. Marriage is a serious business. It is something you should think over and plan about. I never marry people in that fashion, at a moment's notice."

"But my feller is a sailor, and his ship sails to-morrow morning," she said. "So we've got ter get married to-night."

"Then you should have come and told me last week," said the minister.

"I do not often marry any one out of the parish, and when I do, I want good notice of the marriage given so that everything can be done in regular form. Why didn't you let me know before?"

The maiden blushed and looked down. "He only axed me ten minutes ago, an' I come as quick as I could," she said.

The minister succeeded in recovering a serious expression before she looked up. "I'm afraid I can't help you out," he said. "It's against my rules to perform a marriage of that sort. There's a sailors' church not far from here. Go down there and perhaps you can get the clergyman to marry you."

The maiden went out regretfully, and Mr. Braunberg-Lichtenstein entered. He bowed with an air of distinction that would have become a duke. "Vill you haf the kindness to do me a great service?" he said. "Mrs. Schwarz and I vill get married, if you be so kind."

"Mrs. Schwarz!" cried the minister. "You wish to marry Mrs. Schwarz!"

"Yes, sie ist vary gut to mir and I haf decided to marry me with her."

"But have you thought it over carefully? She is much older than you; she belongs to another race. Do you think you will be happy together?"

"Yes, I tink, I like her vary mooch."

The minister did all he could to convince the German that the match would be an unfortunate one, but his words were useless. The strange couple had made up their minds.

Before many days had passed, the widow arrayed in a bridal dress adorned with many flowers, stood proudly by the side of the elegant young German officer, and became by sanction of the law Mrs. Johnson-Schwarz-Braunberg-Lichtenstein.

It was some weeks later that she sought the Lady of Good Cheer in much agitation, hatless and dishevelled.

"My husband!" she cried. "He is gone! I can't find him anywhere!"

"What?" cried the Lady of Good Cheer. "What has happened?"

"Well, you see he's been going uptown every day, and he told me he had work in a restaurant in 42nd Street. But he kept askin' me for money, and tellin' me he couldn't get no pay till Saturday. An' I thinks to meself, 'There's somethin' queer about this business,' and Saturday I puts on me hat and up I goes to the restaurant. Never a sign of Hans could I find, and what's more, they'd never even heard of him. And thinks I, 'There's a woman at the bottom of this and I'll find out about it yet.' When he comes home he gives me a song and dance about their not payin' off till Monday after all, and he wants some money to fix up for Sunday. So I gives him a dollar and thinks I, 'I'll catch you this time.' Well, Sunday evenin' he says, 'I think I'll go up town to the Madison Square Church to-night.' And I says, 'All right.' An when he goes, I slips on me hat and follows him. He stops at a flower store and buys a bouquet, and I thinks, 'Now I'll get you for sure.' Well, he takes the elevated uptown, and I slips in behind without him seein' me. Sure enough he got out at 23rd Street, and I followed him over to Madison Square, and in he goes to the church. Well, I begun to think I was fooled, but I went in too. He met a swell young feller there and the two of 'em sat together. I waited till after the service, and he comes out with the young man and they walks up Fifth Av'noo, arm in arm together, him with his bouquet still in his hand. They turns into 35th Street, and walks to a house half down the block and goes in. Well, it was cold and beginnin' to rain, but I went across the street and leaned up against a railin' and waited. In about an hour he comes out, without the flowers, and he walks over to the L very quick. I follows him. He got out at Chatham Square, and started to walk home. It was late then, pretty near midnight, and I comes up behind him, sudden like, and takes him by the arm and says, kind of quiet like:

'What did ye do with them flowers?' Well, he jumped. He was some surprised, I tell you. 'Yes,' I says, 'I saw you go into that house in 35th Street. What did ye do with them flowers?' 'I give them to a gentleman friend of mine,' he says. 'Go on,' says I. 'Don't tell me no lies! You've been lyin' to me straight every day. You ain't been to work at no restaurant. Here I've took all me savin's to fix you up, and I've give you money every day and you go a spendin' of it on flowers fer some woman up town, and give me a handful of lies about workin' and gettin' your pay. Now you've got to cut it out and get to work, or there'll be trouble.' Well he says there wan't no woman and he left the flowers with a gentleman friend and he's goin' to work Monday. And this morning he's gone with all the spare cash in the house, and I can't find a trace of him nowhere."

Indeed, Mr. Braunberg-Lichtenstein proved to be as irrevocably lost as any of the previous incumbents whose name the much-married woman had borne, and who had been snatched from her by the hand of death. Her grief over his departure, though less decorously expressed, was possibly more poignant than that which she had felt for Mr. Schwarz. To do her justice, however, it should be stated that she sorrowed, not so much because he was lost, as because he had ever been found. She sought to eliminate every trace of his incumbency from her mental horizon, and so, embittered by her fourfold widowhood, she ruthlessly cut off the two latest additions to her cognomen, although she had borne them for a month with great pride. Thenceforward only those who were willing to face a whirlwind of vituperation ventured to salute her as Mrs. Johnson-Schwarz Braunberg-Lichtenstein. It was possibly in the effort to acquire a clear and unencumbered title that in the spring she married a man with the simple name of Smith.

VII

THE GREY DRESS

"HEY, Tim! git on ter de fancy washerlady dey've got in dis yere pallis!" shouted a ragged youngster with a bundle of papers under his arm. He had just deposited one of them in a narrow court surrounded on all sides by the tall tenements of Cherry Hill. At his summons Tim's mop of tow-coloured hair appeared at the opening of the tunnel-like passage beneath the tenements which was the sole entrance to the court. Like the typical New York newsboy that he was, Tim expressed his quick appreciation of the crux of a dilemma by shouting: "Get a wife! Get a wife!" In a moment both boys had vanished through the tunnel as swiftly as they appeared. The "Washerlady" thus saluted straightened herself with some difficulty and stood erect by her tubs with lather covered arms, and as she turned, the newsboy's jeer was readily explained. The quick eyes of the urchin had seen the face whose large drooping moustaches indicated that this was no woman, but a man arrayed in a long apron.

A more serious person than the newsboy might well have smiled at the pathetic incongruity of this round masculine countenance above the foaming tubs. The face had been that of a rubicund, snub-nosed, Teutonic peasant, but hunger and sickness had left a pale shadow on the ruddy cheeks, so that he looked like an old Franz Hals over whose vivid tones some unfeeling hand had put a coat of white-wash. He was about to dive into his suds again after his interruption, when a sound came to him from the open window of the tumble-down rear house behind him, and shaking the lather from his hands, he turned and hurried in at the open door. On the broken lounge by the window lay the frail figure of a woman. Her face was ghastly pale. Her hand clutched her breast, and beneath it a red stain was spreading over the white kerchief. He stood for a moment silent, his piglike little eyes wide and staring, seeing nothing but the white face and the scarlet stain. He groaned, and she turned and saw him. She hid her face quickly so that it should not tell him the depths of her suffering.

"Never mind me," she said. "You must finish them napkins or we'll lose the job."

The man stood watching her a moment, breathing heavily with an asthmatic wheeze. His pale blue eyes filled and a drop trickled down his red nose. Then he shook his head slowly, turned and went out, and without a word plunged once more into the lather, wheezing and groaning like a decrepit donkey engine as he worked.

Then the Lady of Good Cheer found them.

She could not restrain a smile as her eyes fell upon the grotesque "washerlady," but her ready sympathy soon detected the tragedy behind the apparent farce. She had soon found her way to the bedside of the wife and was doing what she could to relieve her paroxysms of pain. The poor woman was more anxious about her napkins than about herself. She and her husband lived upon the income she derived from her position as washerwoman for a Bowery restaurant. It was an income that to the sick woman seemed truly munificent. She received ten cents a hundred for the napkins she washed. Now she would forfeit her position if they were not ready on time, and she would undoubtedly have been more at ease if the Lady of Good Cheer had deserted her to attend to the napkins. Her one idea seemed to be to make her visitor appreciate her husband's efforts at the tubs, and the devotion he showed in doing a woman's work for the sake of keeping her position.

The Lady of Good Cheer assured her that the napkins would be finished on time, and she breathed a sigh of relief. She was sure that at last she had the ear of a woman who would understand, and began to tell all the anxieties and worries that for want of outlet had been eating into her lonely soul. The forlorn pair had had a són who had found riches in America and had sent to Germany for his parents. When they arrived in the new land, he had strangely disappeared. She thought him dead and she and her husband had ever since been struggling desperately for a livelihood, sinking lower and lower as the man became crippled with rheumatism and helpless with asthma. The woman seemed to find the relief that comes from opening a long festering wound as she poured out a story of their despair and shame. Months of sickness and poverty had been made wretched and shameful by drinking and quarrelling in this miserable environment. At home they had been honest, industrious folk; they had done their duty by God and their neighbour. But here in their loneliness and want they had lost all faith and all hope. They drank to forget, and little by little they sank to the level of the degraded life about them.

When the Lady of Good Cheer went away, she left behind her the confidence that somehow life would be better now. She sent in food and a nurse, but the reports she received were not encouraging. The poor woman was in the grip of a deadly disease from which all escape seemed hopeless. Everything possible was done to relieve her, and for a short time she was able to return to her tub. The Lady of Good Cheer visited her constantly and watched her anxiously, but hardly a month had passed when she found Mrs. Reichert lying almost unconscious at her work with the red stain again upon the kerchief at her breast.

When the Lady of Good Cheer spoke of the hospital, she shook her head. In broken words and gasps she explained that she could not leave her home.

"Dese mens! vot can dey do by demselves?" she asked. "Ven I leaf him my man was like a shicken mitout no head, already!" and she smiled a little in spite of her pain.

The washerwoman was deaf to all persuasion. That work at the tub in front of the dilapidated rear tenement was to her a solemn trust. She felt that there the battle for her home and her husband and her self-respect must be fought out.

As the Lady of Good Cheer later told the story of this pale and wrinkled old woman with her torn skirts looped up in her assault upon a foaming wash-tub full of cheap napkins, there was an epic quality in the account that was truly Homeric. Day after day the woman stood at her post. Day after day she rubbed away, gritting her yellow, broken teeth that she might not scream with the pain, and seeking to hide from her husband the red stain on her breast that was always growing larger. All the while the terrible disease was eating her life away, and she knew that certain defeat was hemming her in, a defeat that she would not acknowledge till the last drop of blood was shed.

It was a few months later that the Lady of Good Cheer entered the dark little room in the rear tenement and found Mrs. Reichert lying on the bed with a pile of napkins beside her and sobbing brokenly because she was too weak to stand. "Now you must let me take care of you," said the Lady of Good Cheer. "I have found a nice home which is not a hospital where you will receive the treatment you need, and I have found another pleasant home where they will take care of your husband, so you need not be anxious about him."

Because she could no longer stand at her post, she suffered the Lady of Good Cheer to take her away to the house of Sister Rose. Sister Rose was a fine-spirited and self-sacrificing woman, who had taken this house in the most wretched street in the city, and had transformed a spot of ugliness and filth into a place of comfort and charm. Now she had opened its doors to any of the unfortunates in the neighbourhood upon whom the deadly disease had laid its hand. There they might stay in pretty airy surroundings with tenderest care until the end came.

In this place of rest the washerwoman was to live through what remained of her struggle. The old man was sent to a pleasant home not far away, where every day he could work in the flower garden as he loved to do, or sit under the trees and smoke his pipe. The Lady of Good Cheer visited them both many times, and her visits were the events to which they looked forward through the monotony of uneventful days.

Through the long months the woman lay on her

bed of torture, waiting the end that she knew must come soon. She did not complain. She was used to hardship, and her gratitude for the little services that were rendered her was pathetic. Slowly she grew feebler until at last she saw that she could not endure many more days of pain. She sent for the Lady of Good Cheer. Her visitor took the sick woman's hand, and felt a half-timid anxiety in her eyes, and a nervous self-consciousness about her that was a new and unexpected element in her simple straightforward character.

"You wanted me? What can I do for you?" asked the Lady of Good Cheer.

The sick woman seemed to be struggling for courage to speak. "You vas always so gut by me. Vill you do von ting yet? Ven I'm gone," she went on unsteadily, "ven I'm tet, you know, vill you tend to eferyting for me? Mein man iss fery veak. He can do notings. Dere vill be plenty moneys, von mein insurance. I haf it always paid; efen ven ve haf no food."

"Of course, I will attend to everything," said the Lady of Good Cheer.

But this did not seem to relieve the sick woman. Her nervousness increased, and a faint flush appeared on her pale cheek.

"What is it?" asked the Lady of Good Cheer gently. "What else can I do?"

"I'm afrait you tink me terrible foolish. Und maybe it vas wrong already."

"Tell me what it is," said the Lady of Good Cheer.

The flush deepened. She looked down and fingered the bedclothes. "Vell," she started, and then broke off suddenly—"Oh, it is so foolish, I got ashame to tell! I vant so much a new dress, not black and sad; I want a grey dress, all pretty mit little lacings like I see Miss Schmidt haf. You tink it iss bad already, ven you take some insurance money and buy dot dress? I vant so long a grey dress," she went on apologetically, "efer since we vas married already. I safe moneys time and time again. Efery time, my man he took sick, or he lose his vork, and I must take dose moneys for him. Now he don't vant no moneys. You tink it fery wrong, I haf dot grey dress after I vas tet?"

The Lady of Good Cheer gasped with astonishment. She had thought she understood this little woman, but here was a new bit of self-revelation. That within the imagination of this forlorn figure, with its torn pinned-up skirts, should have been hidden a vision of feminine vanities seemed a paradox too absurd to be real. The Lady of Good Cheer had appreciated the courage of the woman as she toiled at her tubs through all those days of cruel suffering; she had supplied her with food and the necessities of life, and it had not occurred to her that there could be in the heart of this worn struggling creature a desire for anything save the crude essentials of life. And yet, all the while that she toiled at the tubs, gaunt, dishevelled, ragged, with raw, blistered hands and white, drawn face, she had not been merely one of the suffering proletariat, poverty-stricken in imagination as well as in estate. She had been a *woman,* who longed to dress up in pretty clothes and be admired by the only man in the world whose opinion mattered. All through those days of cruel toil she had actually been planning how she could save enough to buy one pretty dress. She had thought it all out,— how she would put it on when her husband was out, and smooth her hair, and fasten a bow at her throat. When he came back how surprised he would look! She would see the old light in his eyes and perhaps he would say, "Ach Lena, wie schön bist du!" But that dream had never come true. Each time when the money was almost saved, sickness came and she was compelled to draw on the little fund of her heart's desire to provide food and comforts for her husband. The pathos of the little woman's life came with new keenness to the Lady of Good Cheer, and the impulse to smile died away in her heart, a sudden sob seemed to catch in her throat.

In the meantime, the sick woman was looking at her visitor anxiously, and at last the Lady of

Good Cheer found voice to say, " Indeed it is right for you to have the grey dress, and I promise you that you shall wear it as you wish."

A shy smile came over the worn face, and she reached out her thin hand and clasped the hand of the Lady of Good Cheer.

" Thank you," she said. " That makes me so happy. You understand, don't you? "

The Lady of Good Cheer kept her promise. When at last rest came to the frail form that had been wounded and torn so terribly by the shattering blows of circumstance, the Lady of Good Cheer folded the sad hands, cracked and worn by hard toil and faithful service, over the bosom of the grey dress. She was surprised to see what a charm there was about the frail little figure in the graceful folds of soft stuff that hid all the unlovely angular lines, and it seemed to her that a shy smile lingered about the lips with the wistful question: " Will he think that I look pretty now? "

As she lay there, a knock came at the door. The old man stood on the threshold with his hands full of beautiful chrysanthemums. " How is she to-day? " he asked. They told him the sad news. He said brokenly: " Tod! Sie ist tod! But dese flowers — vot can I do mit diesen Blumen? I haf planted dem de first day as I come to dot home. She luf dem flowers so mooch. Efery day I watch dem, an' I say, 'Soon I bring dem mit to her.' Dey vas shoost for her. To-day dey vas ready, und I bring dem quick, und now —" and he hid his face behind the blossoms.

They told him to lay the flowers gently on the folds of the grey dress, and the old man turned away comforted. "She look so happy," he said. "I tink she know I bring dem flowers."

The next week, when the Lady of Good Cheer gathered her group of mothers as usual at the appointed hour, one of the women rose. "I went to see Mrs. Reichert at Sister Rose's house just the day before she died," she said, "and she says to me, 'Will you do something for me when I'm gone, Mrs. Mack?' says she; and I says, 'You'll not be goin' for a long time yet, Mrs. Reichert.' And she says, 'Yes, I'm goin'. Last night I was sleepin' and I heard some one callin' me. I looked up and — Oh! I can't tell you all I seen! But He was there; and He says, "Come," with His hand stretched out to me just like the picture. And it's all right, and I'm so happy! It's all the Lady of Good Cheer,' she says, 'if it hadn't been for her, I don't know what would have become of me! I've tried to thank her, but I can't. I feel so foolish when she's lookin' at me. I've been thinkin' and thinkin' how I can thank her, and I want you to go to the meeting, and when it's time for the verses, you tell them you've got a verse to read for me. I think she'd like a verse better than anything, just as if I was there in my place at the meeting. And then,' says she, 'you say to the Lady of Good Cheer: "Inasmuch as ye did it unto the least of these, ye did it unto Me."'"

VIII

A LOST SOUL

THE Lady of Good Cheer stood hesitating in front of a strange building on the corner of Hamilton Street. The building was locally known as "The Ship." This appellation, though apparently innocent, had not sufficed to give the house a good name in the neighbourhood, for its nautical associations were piratical rather than commercial. Hitherto the Lady of Good Cheer had passed by the house as a place of ill omen, and it had taken a special invitation to bring her to its doors. The day before, when she was out on her round of calls, she had encountered a figure so extraordinary and quaint that it seemed to have been cut from some old time story book. An ancient dame, bent almost double and leaning on a heavy cane, came hobbling towards her, and screwing her head sideways, had peered up at her and begged for alms. Her face was deeply wrinkled; a long nose and projecting chin threatened to meet over her sunken mouth and thick lips. Her hair beneath the queer peaked bonnet, was snowy white, and with her short skirt, black apron and buckled shoes, she was so exactly the figure of which every child has dreamed, that the Lady of

Good Cheer would scarcely have been surprised if she had flown away on a broomstick. The Lady of Good Cheer gave no alms, but asked the old dame for her address, and promised to call and see if she could render any service. When she looked up the number given her, she found herself in front of "The Ship."

"The Ship" was a most surprising building to encounter in the centre of a great modern city. It was situated on one of the narrowest, darkest lanes in the ward. All that could be seen of it from the street was a low battered wall, with here and there a shattered window, and above an incoherent jumble of roofs of different lengths and styles, and with a multitude of angles.

The Lady of Good Cheer made an end of hesitation by entering the low wooden door, and passing through a narrow, crooked hall into a quaint old court paved with stone. It was doubtless from this court that the building derived its name, though there was a tradition that the name was due to the fact that it had been built from the timbers of a ship. A low gallery surrounded the court at about the height of a man's head. It was roofed over and railed in like a ship's deck, and upon it opened a row of doors like so many cabins. A number of crooked companionways led up to this balcony, and from it on to other galleries and half floors, for only a few square feet of the ramshackle building seemed to be on one level. To get anywhere, one had to go up two steps or to go down three steps. Inside the halls were so narrow and crooked and dark and the stairs so winding and broken that it seemed like a veritable labyrinth. The building was all of wood and in order to increase the rent, one room after another had been added on, like patches on an old garment. Every possible corner had been roofed in, every available nook projected into a room, and every tiny room was occupied by a large family. The court of the balconies or main hatch was full of ragged little imps and disreputable hags, and at night screams and curses echoed from the dry old rafters and reverberated in the black winding halls, till it seemed like some ancient hulk haunted by demons and filled with tortured souls.

The Lady of Good Cheer looked about the dark court-yard for some traces of the old woman. Underneath the balcony was a row of doors the bottoms of which were below the level of the stone court, and little flights of broken steps led down to the cellar rooms into which they opened. These rooms were all occupied by families who paid a cheap rent of only four or five dollars a month. The Lady of Good Cheer descended one of these flights of steps and knocked at the door. She entered a damp room dimly lighted by one window beneath the balcony. There was the usual necessary furniture, a stove, a table, two chairs, an old wardrobe, and in a tiny adjoining closet, a bed. In a dilapidated rocking-chair the old crone sat, bending forward and leaning her folded hands on her stick. In the dim light little of her face was visible save the long, hooked nose and projecting chin, and a glimmer of silver hair. She mumbled a greeting with toothless jaws; the Lady of Good Cheer felt more than ever that she was playing a leading rôle in some drama of enchantment.

"How are you getting on, Mrs. Wiggins?" she asked cheerily.

"Not so well now, Mum. Things is werry bad with me now. You wouldn't think to look at me that my cousin is Lord Treasurer of the Dominion of Canada, would you? But he is, and he's werry good to me. He sends me a letter with a check every now and then. Here's one now with the crown and all on it."

She handed the Lady of Good Cheer the letter with the insignia of a well known family upon it. The letter was a kindly one expressing a desire to do something for a poor and distant relative who apparently had no real claim.

"How did you get into such trouble, if you belong to such a good family?" asked the Lady of Good Cheer, sympathetically.

The old woman lifted her head a little, and with her little eyes blinking behind thick glasses and a crooked forefinger extended, she croaked: "Strange things happen in this world," she said.

"Things you wouldn't never believe," and her voice sunk to a hoarse whisper.

Just at that moment from the dark recesses of the room came a low moan. It was so uncanny and unexpected that the Lady of Good Cheer started involuntarily.

"What is that?" she cried.

"Oh, that's nothing," said the old woman. "I often hear that. Yes, yes, there's a lot o' trouble in this world, and them that's rich never knows how they'll end."

Just then came another groan so forlorn and so desperate that the Lady of Good Cheer sprang to her feet.

"There is something in this room!" she cried.

"Yes," said the old woman cautiously, "perhaps there is."

The moan came again, this time unmistakable: "I'm lost! I'm lost!" it wailed.

The Lady of Good Cheer stepped swiftly toward the wardrobe in the dark corner. The tall chest was so narrow it seemed impossible that any human being could be hiding there. She seized the handle of the wardrobe door, and was about to throw it wide open, when suddenly some unseen force snatched the door from her grasp and closed it with a bang.

She felt a real thrill of horror. To feel a door torn from one's hands by an unknown agency is enough to make the flesh creep. The Lady of

Good Cheer was not superstitious, and as she stood there in the black corner, ghostly fright soon changed to a more serious fear. Was this old crone really concealing some crime in her dark cellar? What wretched creature was imprisoned here in the darkness? All manner of horrible possibilities rose before her as she struggled with the door, while the old woman still rocked on and mumbled. The chill of the damp cellar seemed to creep over her as she felt the door resist her renewed effort to fling it open. It seemed as if some blood-curdling nightmare were making itself real before her eyes. What awful Thing was behind that door? It scarcely seemed possible that it was human. The Lady of Good Cheer had no place in her mind for superstitious fears, and refused to be daunted by hideous realities. She gave a final tug at the door. It gave way, and she sprang back in sudden horror. There, all huddled in a heap in the dark bottom of the wardrobe, she could just distinguish a human body, unclothed, smeared with dirt and partly covered by long tangled hair. But before she could cry out, the body, wedged in the narrow space, moved and seemed about to sit up. She saw under the tangle of hair the glint of two eyes fixed upon her, and she heard a low, moaning wail. "Let me alone!" the Thing cried. "I'm lost!"

It took but a moment for the Lady of Good Cheer to recover from the shock of her discovery, and to realise that this was no hallucination but a tragic reality, a human creature in distress. She turned to the old woman in indignation. "What is this?" she asked.

"Hush!" answered the woman in a whisper. "It's my sister, Violet. She's not right here," and she pointed to her head. "Come away: you can't do anything. She thinks she's done wrong, and that her soul is lost, poor thing!"

The door was suddenly shut again, and again that wail sounded: "I'm lost! I'm lost!"

The Lady of Good Cheer knelt by the wardrobe door, and tried to calm the wretched creature within. As a mother would speak to a terrified child, she sought to soothe the pain of the tortured soul. Her only answer was a broken, hopeless sob. The poor brain was too muddled to grasp the meaning of her words. It only understood in some vague way the thrill of sympathy in the voice, and felt that here was a friend.

After a time the nurse, whom the Lady of Good Cheer sent in to look after the unfortunate Violet, succeeded in placing the woman in a home where she received proper care. Mrs. Wiggins bitterly resented all attempts to place her in an Old Ladies' Home, and "stuck to 'The Ship'" with true Anglo-Saxon stubbornness. Violet slowly regained her mind, but the old lady died in the damp, dirty corner of the house of many gables and angles and windings that had been so appropriate a setting for her while she lived. "The Ship" itself was finally torn down. The Lady of Good Cheer many times recalled the shock of horror she received on her first visit to the place, as she watched the queer courts and ancient roofs give way before a huge modern tenement, whose cheaply ornamented walls of yellow brick were hideous enough to drive the old-style hobgoblins from the neighbourhood forever.

IX

THE LOST BATTLE

THE Lady of Good Cheer and the minister with several members of the choir were scaling the dark stairway of a Catherine Street tenement.

"I hope Mr. Schweizer won't make any trouble," she said. "He hates the church and all religious services, but Mrs. Schweizer was so anxious to have a service before her little boy was buried that I told her we would come. Mr. Schweizer has been drinking and I am afraid he may be disagreeable. He treats her terribly. I know he struck her only the other day."

They knocked at a door on the third floor and entered a pretty little apartment where a number of people were assembled. They were grouped about a table, on which lay a tiny coffin banked with flowers. As they entered a short man with a heavy jaw and black moustache stepped forward.

"What's this?" he cried thickly. "I don't want none of your psalm-singing in here! Get out, all of you!"

"Oh, Fritz!" called a soft voice from behind, "don't talk like that! I asked them to come. I won't let little Henry be carried away and buried without a prayer — it's heathen. Come now!

You've had your way in everything. Let me do what I want with my own child."

A slender, graceful woman, scarce more than a girl, stepped up beside him. There was a delicate piquancy about the face beneath its heavy black veil that made one start and wonder if perhaps some fair flower from the Court of Versailles had stepped upon a magic carpet and been carried away and hidden in this tenement. There was an exquisite daintiness about her, in the poise of her head, in the shell pink colouring of her cheek, in the coquettish coil of her gold-brown hair, and in the delicate chiseling of her red lips, that made her seem most out of place here among the tenements. The refinement of her appearance was startlingly emphasised as she stood beside the intoxicated man with his sodden features, and tried to smother his raucous curses with her swift words. It was a strange conflict, that of this fragile and delicate girl mother with the drunken brute of a father over the tiny baby form that lay there embowered in roses. The man was deaf to the sacred appeal of the moment and insensible to common decency, but she won the day. There was a compelling nobility about her which even he could not resist, and before he knew it, he found himself shifted dexterously to the background, while she was saying to the minister: "Don't mind him! He doesn't know what he is saying. I'm sorry he was so rude."

In another moment she had pushed her husband gently into a seat where he remained muttering angrily with half-glazed eyes. Then she came forward to greet her guests. "Come right in!" she said. "We're all ready for the service. It was so good of you to come."

The little group from the church entered and stood together around the small white coffin on its bed of flowers. As they sang the familiar hymns, the young mother held in her lap her other child, a boy of three, and sobbed softly, while in the distance the muttered curses of her husband sounded a low, growling accompaniment. As the minister started to read the solemn words of the funeral service, he was startled by a shout and a sudden commotion, and the mother gave a faint cry as she saw her husband stagger to his feet.

"Well, I'm not going to stay and listen to that stuff!" cried the man with a snarl, and he flung out of the room, slamming the door with a bang.

The service ended with another hymn, and there was no further interruption. The Lady of Good Cheer stopped afterward to say what she could to comfort Mrs. Schweizer. It was the first death in the little family circle, and the young wife was broken-hearted by her husband's behaviour.

"I don't know what we shall do," she said. "He does nothing but drink all the time. He can't do any work. He's really sick, too, and that's one reason he drinks. He knows it's killing him, but he says he can't stop. Can't you get Mr. Day to come in and talk to him? Perhaps he could get him to go away to some cure. We can't go on living like this. It's just killing me."

The Lady of Good Cheer gave her the sympathy she needed, and assured her that Mr. Day, the assistant minister, would see her husband and make some arrangement for his welfare. The young wife bade her good-bye with many expressions of gratitude, and went back to her dead child.

Some months later the Lady of Good Cheer entered the tunnel that led beneath one of the ancient houses of Cherry Hill. She passed through a long dark passage, and came out in a narrow court surrounded by wretched tumbledown tenements. Six of these miserable habitations, each more forlorn than the last, opened on the little court. A crowd of ragged little Italians were playing in the yard, a drunken Irishman lay on one of the door steps, and several slatternly figures could be seen watching her from doorway and window. On the lines across the yard a startling variety of clothing was hung out to dry. Gay Italian scarfs, torn white skirts, red petticoats, yellow comfortables were arrayed together on one line, waving like the flags of all nations spread to catch the breeze.

Photo by J. H. Denison.

REAR COURT ON CHERRY HILL

The Lady of Good Cheer turned into the most wretched barracks of them all. She climbed the broken front steps and entered a hall redolent of garlic and stale macaroni, and oppressive in the heat of summer with the sickening odours of decay. She held her breath as she passed by open doors. Through one door she could see a ragged, drunken Irishman who was shouting curses and shaking his fist at a dirty wife. Another door revealed a room crowded with Italians of all sizes and ages, all of them unspeakably dirty and squalid in appearance. She knocked at the door at the back, and a clear sweet voice called, "Come in." She entered and found herself in a wretched little room with bare, wooden walls and floor and a low, uneven ceiling. The furniture in the room was neat and pretty, however: a large bed covered with a white bedspread, a polished stove, a handsome table and a few well-made chairs. In the middle of the floor knelt Mrs. Schweizer, a full length apron drawn over her neat black skirt. Her sleeves were rolled up, showing her beautiful white arms, and she had a scrubbing brush in her hand and a pail of suds at her side. Her cheeks were flushed, and a lock of her shining chestnut hair had escaped from its smooth coils and hung in a charmingly defiant little curl over her white neck. She looked up at the Lady of Good Cheer with consternation in her eyes.

"Oh, excuse me!" she said, trying to master

the vagrant lock. "I look like a perfect fright. I had no idea it was you."

The Lady of Good Cheer assured her that she had never looked better, but the little woman continued: "You see, I'm just back from work and I have to pitch in and clean up, for the house is a sight after Willie has been playing around all day. I've got to wash him up next," she added, with a glance at a pretty little boy, whose neat dress showed traces of the day's vigorous campaign for amusement.

"Do you leave him here all day?" asked the Lady of Good Cheer.

"I have to, you see!" Mrs. Schweizer answered. "I'm working in a restaurant in Park Row, and it's hard work. I run in at noon for a minute to give him his lunch and see how he's getting on, and then I come back at night and clean up and get him his supper. It's terribly hard to leave him all day in this place. The people are awfully rough. I'm frightened about him all day long, and every night I come home with my heart in my mouth for fear I'll find him sick or dead or something — but what can I do?"

"What do you hear from Mr. Schweizer?"

"Oh, he's getting on splendidly out in that Home in Colorado. He's stopped drinking entirely and he's getting over the consumption."

"That is splendid. I am so glad," said the Lady of Good Cheer. "But I'm afraid this work is too hard for you. It is too much to work all day and look out for your house too."

"It *is* hard. I have to stand all day washing dishes, and some of these awfully hot days it was so close in there next the stove, I thought I should faint. I am so tired at night, I can hardly get home. You see, I'm not used to work like that."

Her deep brown eyes were full of tears now, and her delicate lips quivered.

"Why don't you go back to your father and mother till Mr. Schweizer comes home, or at least ask them for help?"

The girl was on her feet now and the graceful little head was held high.

"No, never!" she said and her eyes flashed through her tears. "You see, they forbade me to marry, and told me I'd get into trouble. No, I've made my bed, and I've got to lie in it now."

She looked so like the Princess of the Fairy Tales in misfortune as she stood there with her flushed and tear-stained cheeks, her proud head held high, defying her fate, that the Lady of Good Cheer was uncertain whether to cry or to applaud.

"But can you make it go, even so?" she asked.

"Yes. They give me six dollars a week at the restaurant, and my rent is only five dollars a month here. And they give me some food at the restaurant too. I always have some cakes to bring home to Willie."

"Do they treat you well there?" asked the Lady of Good Cheer.

"Oh, some of them are pretty rough, but the boss — well, he treats me almost too well," she said, and her delicate cheek flushed suddenly a deeper scarlet. "Oh," she cried suddenly, "do you know how hard it is to stick it out and do right, when I could have anything I want for myself and the boy, if I —" she burst suddenly into tears. "Sometimes I think I'll go mad," she said. "I am so worried about Willie, and the work is so hard, I think I'll drop dead before I get back. And then to come back to this place, with all these awful people around —" She shuddered convulsively.

"Mrs. Schweizer," said the Lady of Good Cheer, "you're the bravest woman I know. I'm proud to have you as my friend and to take your hand. I do know just how hard a fight it is, and I'm afraid I shouldn't be half as brave as you are. I shall think of you every day, and if ever you need me, if ever I can be of the least help, I'll come to you no matter what I am doing. You'll call on me, won't you? It would make me so happy to do even a little to help."

The tears had ceased now. She stood very quiet and pale with her head still proudly erect.

"There's nothing you or any one else can do. I've made a mistake with my life and I've got to work it out, all alone, no matter how hard it is.

I can do it, I know, only sometimes I get discouraged. When they are at you all the time,— when you think how easy it might be,— well, it's hard sometimes."

The Lady of Good Cheer went away saddened and anxious. How long could a delicate frame stand the test of hard labour, cruel anxiety, foul surroundings, and the constant pressure of insidious temptation?

A year passed, and it was time for Mr. Schweizer to return. The Lady of Good Cheer rejoiced that the long period of cruel toil and dragging weeks was over. Mrs. Schweizer had moved, and the Lady of Good Cheer went in to congratulate her on the good news. As she knocked at the door, a well dressed man opened it and came out. She entered and found herself in a pleasant, prettily furnished apartment, a marked contrast to the wretched room in Cherry Street. A can of beer and two empty glasses stood on the table. Mrs. Schweizer rose to meet her. The Lady of Good Cheer noticed that she wore a striking dress with brilliant dashes of red about it, and she felt the greeting die away on her lips as she looked at the woman before her. The delicate face had grown cold and hard. An inscrutable veil seemed to have been drawn over the soft, brown eyes. The exquisite colour of the cheek had changed to a harsh flush, and the lips had coarse lines about them. The Lady of Good

Cheer felt a false timbre, a cold defiance, in the voice that she remembered as one of unusual sweetness. She could only murmur a few commonplaces in response to the woman's greeting; she wanted to escape and indulge in an old fashioned cry. She made a hurried excuse and turned away, and all the way home the hot tears stung her eyelids and a sob was gripping at her throat. "I might have done no better in her place," she kept thinking. "But if I could only have helped her a little more — only one month more. Now it is too late."

X

A CRUEL DILEMMA

THERE is a spirit of neighbourliness even in the huge tenement barracks where physical necessity rubs men's noses together in such close contact that the instinct of their souls is to retire in sheer revulsion to the greatest possible distance from one another. It was this spirit which called the attention of the Lady of Good Cheer to the " lady up on the top floor " who was " terrible sick, and didn't have no one so much as to pass the time o' day with her while her man was away to work." This was the top floor of a tenement which was perhaps the most wretched of the many crowded tenements in the " Long Block." It provided apartments consisting of a kitchen and dark bedroom for a cheap rent, and in its dark hall one was continually bumping into the most unsavoury and disreputable representatives of every nation.

In response to the spirit of neighbourliness of the " lady " on the first floor, the Lady of Good Cheer climbed to the top story and knocked at the left hand door in front. Her knock was answered by a deep voice that sounded more like a hail from a fishing smack off the Labrador coast, than a summons to enter a Cherry Street tenement.

She was greeted, as she entered, by a stout, quaint figure that spoke of oilskins and sou'wester and spray-drenched decks and wriggling cod. His weather-beaten face was seamed with many a kindly wrinkle. He wore a white goatee, and his hair was grey and worn away from his forehead, but he had a rugged vigour, a quick energetic way of moving, and a forceful method of speech that promised for many years to come, the capacity for hard labour. He had been sitting beside a bed upon which a woman was lying. They had moved the bed out from the dark bedroom, where there was no light and air, and placed it beside the window in the front room. The woman was very ill. Her thin face was white and drawn, save when an unnatural flush burned on her cheek. She seemed to be gasping for breath.

"Oh, you're the lady from the church," said the man with a strong New England twang. "The old woman's pretty bad. Don't ye think so? Eh?"

"She does look very sick," said the Lady of Good Cheer. "I see you've been taking good care of her. It's good that you could get off from work to be with her."

"Well, I dunno *as* it is, an' I dunno as it *is*," said the old man. "That's as you looks at it. There ain't much money fallin' down the chimbly while I set here. But somehow I can't go off t' work with her lyin' here and gaspin'. I went down to the ship and started in unloadin', but I got t' thinkin' o' her lyin' up here all alone and gaspin' fer breath, and I had ter knock off. Couldn't stand it, ye know."

The Lady of Good Cheer went over to the bedside and spoke her sympathy, as she patted the pillow and gave to the bed the little touches of comfort which a woman's hand knows instinctively. Then she sat down, leaning one elbow upon the bed, and bending over to catch the laboured speech of the sick woman. It was not the words which the Lady of Good Cheer brought to her sick that comforted them. She gave them herself,—her strength of will, her courage and faith, her peace of mind. The words were commonplace enough, but a strong will spoke through them, and there was a light of divine sympathy in her eyes, and an assurance of divine restfulness in every gesture and tone, that brought to the pain-racked woman the vision of overshadowing wings of love.

When the Lady of Good Cheer turned to go, the old man followed her into the hall.

"She looks wretchedly feeble," she said. "What does she get to eat?"

"Wall, she ain't sick from over feedin'," the old man jerked out, with a quick sideways glance from beneath his bushy eyebrows.

"I'm afraid you yourself haven't had enough to eat while you have been away from work," said the Lady of Good Cheer looking at him closely.

"Wall," said the old man shamefacedly and hanging his head. "I hate to own it an' I'd never speak for meself, but we ain't had a scrap of vittles in the house for two days, and I'm that weak I couldn't do no work if I tried. But what kin I do," he went on with a scowl of perplexity that overshadowed his keen blue eyes. "She mought die any minute, an' I can't leave her lyin' here all alone, coughin' and gaspin', with no one but them dirty drunken Irish around. I can't do it, it's no use o' talkin'; an' if I don't work, there's no money comin' in, and nawthin' ter eat."

A tear came unbidden, and trickled slowly down the weather-beaten cheek. He drew the back of his hand roughly across his eyes. "I'd orter be ashamed o' meself," he said, "but I'm plum discouraged. It don't seem hardly right somehow. I've been a good livin' man, and I've allers done me best, an' me an' her has lived together nigh onter forty years, and now I've either got ter leave her ter suffer and die all alone, or else I've got ter set still here an' see her starve ter death. I was readin' in the papers yesterday as how one o' them rich fellers on Fifth Avenue spent ten thousand dollars just fer posies fer his dinner party, an' if I had just ten dollars, it'd save the old woman from starvin'. An' I was readin' how one o' them rich women spent hundreds o' dollars fittin' out a puppy dog. I've allers been a hard workin' man and never shirked me work, an' it don't seem right. I s'pose you think there's a God, but it don't seem no use ter pray, ner nothin'."

A sudden fierce light came into his keen eyes. "Sometimes when I see her lyin' there an' starvin' so patient like, I feel's if I'd like ter get a gun and go up an' shoot some o' them rich fellers, and take enough to keep the old woman alive. What do they care fer us folks? They ain't any o' them worked harder'n I have. It ain't right, I tell yer, it ain't right."

It was a hard problem to solve. The Lady of Good Cheer felt a fierce anger spring up in her breast. It seemed as if some cruel Demon controlled the economic conditions of the world, gathering where he had not strewn, leaving the faithful workers to starve in anguish, while the indolent and selfish flourished. But she only said: "It is terrible indeed, but I believe God has sent me to help you, and I will see that your wife gets the care and food she needs. I will send some one in to sit with her while you are away. Where do you work? Is it far away?"

"I'm workin' 'long shore now. I uster have a ship oncet, but I had bad luck and lost her in a storm, and since then I've had to turn to and work with them drunken Irish loafers on the dock."

The Lady of Good Cheer reached out and took his gnarled and weather-beaten hand in her own slender one, and spoke with quiet positiveness: "It does seem as if the whole world was against you, and I don't blame you a bit for feeling as you do. But behind all that seems so cruel and hard is a greater purpose and a greater love than we can understand. Don't doubt that. God is caring for you even now, and in the end he will set things right."

The strength of her conviction spoke in every word, and her deep set eyes had in them a compelling intensity. The man could not but feel and believe that those eyes saw what was hidden to him.

"Wall, I hope so!" he said. "I've allus b'lieved in God, an' down in me old home in Maine I uster go to church, but in this place it seems as if there wa'n't no God."

He stood silent a moment, his weatherbeaten features working as he sought to keep back the tears. He turned to go back to his place beside the dying woman, and said slowly: "But it ain't in reason the Lord sh'd git a man inter sich a fix that he's got ter leave his wife to die alone like a dog, or else set by her and starve. Mebbe the Lord did send ye ter fix things up — mebbe He did. I'm bound ter b'lieve He did."

XI

A DOMESTIC CRISIS

THE little home into which the Lady of Good Cheer had just made an entrance was a well furnished one on the top story of a queer three cornered tenement in New Chambers Street. It was never uncomfortably immaculate, but there was about it ordinarily an atmosphere of geniality and good cheer. This agreeable atmosphere was created chiefly by the activity of the mistress, a pretty and capable little lady from Paris whose bright dark eyes, smooth red cheeks, and expressive little mouth with full red lips were sufficiently attractive to make one overlook the fact that her figure was too much inclined to embonpoint to meet the sylph-like standards of Parisian beauty. Now, however, the busy housekeeper had been reduced to helplessness by the cruel necessities of motherhood. She lay weak and sick in the bedroom, and her large family of children, who possessed the full measure of Gallic vivacity plus the exhilaration of the atmosphere of the Land of the Free, had played leap frog with the furniture, and left dishes and kitchen utensils in picturesque confusion. Her husband, a short stolid little Frenchman, with a round handsome face, and sad dark eyes, sat dejectedly by the kitchen table with his head sunk on his breast, his long dark hair mussed distractedly on his forehead. He scarcely looked up at the greeting of the Lady of Good Cheer.

"Ah, vat sall I do?" he said. "I cannot get ze work. Zey want men no more to make ze slippers by ze hand. Zey make zem all by ze machine, and ze cheeldren have nossing to eat, and now here ees come anosser bébé!"

It was indeed a sad situation for the Le Boutilliers. The Lady of Good Cheer had been called into see them some months before during the sickness of a little girl. The child had died in spite of all that could be done, but by her constant, sympathetic and watchful care the Lady of Good Cheer had completely won the affection of these warmhearted foreigners, who felt themselves desperately alone in the strange city. Le Boutillier was a skilled workman, who was very clever at making slippers and shoes by hand, but lately machines had been introduced which threw him and his fellow workmen entirely out of employment. If he did get any work he had to compete with the machine-made product, and his best efforts would not bring in more than four dollars a week.

Mrs. Le Boutillier was a marvel as a housekeeper. She had won a prize at the church for the most skilful use of a dollar in the purchase of food. The housekeepers from uptown who saw the results of her expenditure were amazed at the completeness and the variety of her exhibition. Nothing was forgotten, not even the pepper and vinegar and oil for the salad dressing. It was a perfectly balanced meal fit for any gourmet, and remarkable for its contrast with the purchases of the Irish housekeepers, who spent half the dollar on tea and the rest on a poor piece of meat, and of the Scotch, who bought with the dollar enough oatmeal and baked beans to last the family a month. But even Mrs. Le Boutillier had to have a dollar to work her magic, and now the dollar was not forthcoming. Besides, one of the children had been desperately ill, and care and medicines had again been required.

The Lady of Good Cheer had secured some milk tickets from the Dispensary, and every day little Gaspard had gone over with a ticket and brought back a can of milk. This experience that milk came from milk tickets resulted in considerable mental confusion when correlated with the pictures of cows in the process of being milked as he had seen them in Kindergarten. Consequently when he first went to the country and saw a cow grazing in the meadows, his muddled apperception crystallised at once under the stimulus of great excitement, and he exclaimed, "Oh, look at that milk ticket!" Gaspard was a stocky little urchin of some seven years, with brown eyes which sparkled with a glint of impish laughter, as if he were rejoicing in the knowledge that there was a cannon cracker about to explode under your chair. He had a firm little mouth, and a curious scar or birthmark on his cheek which added to the satirical and Puck-like expression of his countenance. The rest of the family were somewhat in awe of little Gaspard. They never knew what new bit of ingenuity would evolve from his sprightly brain.

Marie, a girl of ten, upon whose shoulders the cares of housekeeping rested during her mother's illness, did not find him of great assistance in washing the dishes, scrubbing the floor, and especially in packing the other children away in their common beds at night. His unwillingness to be thus compressed at bed time may have been due to his recent experience of spending two weeks in the country. On the first night of his vacation, when his wriggling members were at last confined in a clean white night suit and he was deposited between the sheets of a pretty little bed, he promptly rolled over to the farthest edge and flattened himself against the wall. He looked back over his shoulder at the crowd of little white clad figures waiting to be located for the night and shouted: "How many of youse is comin' in here?"

The teacher answered: "No one is coming in, Gaspard. The bed is just for you." Gaspard rose to his knees and stared with his eyes as big as saucers.

"De whole bed!" he cried. "Gee! See me

flop!" And he threw himself flat face down with arms and legs expanded to their utmost radius like a human starfish.

Gaspard was standing near Mr. Le Boutillier as the Lady of Good Cheer entered. After she had sought to remove from the father's brow the cloud of melancholy which the arrival of his latest born had occasioned, Gaspard led her into the bedroom where Mrs. Le Boutillier lay, pale but smiling, with a fine fat blue-eyed baby at her side.

"Ees he not a fine bébé?" the mother asked, looking down at him tenderly. "But," she went on, glancing up with an apologetic smile, "what we sall do, me, I know not. How we can get ze food for one more? My husband, he ees so trouble. Ze children, zay have nossing to eat all day. Ah, poor little bébé, zay none of zem wants you, none but me!" And she pressed the little head against her cheek and her eyes filled with tears which trickled down on to the face of the child until he rolled his blue eyes in astonishment.

All the twinkle was gone from Gaspard's face. He looked solemn and old, with his firm little lips and the scar on his cheek and a wrinkle on his brow.

"But, Mother," he said, "why did you go and get another baby when there ain't enough in the house for the kids you've got? Me and Marie haven't had but an old dry bit of bread all day, and when we keep askin' father to give us somethin' to eat, he just sits there and shakes his head and says he can't get no work. Wot cher goin' ter do when that kid gets hungry and begins to howl?"

Mrs. Le Boutillier for answer only pressed the babe closer and began to sob. Gaspard looked conscience-stricken when he saw his mother's tears.

"Aw, say!" he said, "don't cry, Mother! I know what we'll do! There's an old feller down the street wants his coal carried up, and I'll go down and carry coal for him. I'm strong,"—and he displayed his little muscles—"I'll bet I can work as well as those old loafers. If I work hard all day he'd orter give me a quarter, hadn't he?" he went on eagerly. "He'd give me ten cents anyway, an' in a week I'd have about a dollar, an' that'll git enough food fer us. So don't you cry, Mother!" and he patted her hand as it lay on the bed beside him.

The Lady of Good Cheer felt a strange clutching at the throat as she listened to this unexpected speech. She knew that here in the Fourth Ward the little ones she loved lived close to the dark shadows and that it could not be long before even the most joyous and careless must feel the chill touch of poverty or death. She had rejoiced in the manly way in which many of the young boys and girls stood up to share the cares of their parents, but there was something about this small imp of mischief as he squared his stout little

Photo by J. H. Denison.

UNDER THE SHADOW

shoulders to the burden of the responsibility which he could only dimly imagine, that seemed unusual even to her and touched her deeply. Mrs. Le Boutillier smiled through her tears.

"Oh, Gaspard!" she said. "You don't understand! We mus' pay for ze bébé."

Gaspard's black eyes opened wide at this unexpected news, but he was not yet disheartened.

"How much yer gotter pay?" he asked. "What does babies cost?"

"I've got to pay ten dollars," said his mother.

"Gee!" said Gaspard, utterly aghast. "It would take me weeks an' weeks to make all that money!"

He stood a moment in silence, bravely concealing his discouragement lest his mother should weep again. Then slowly he picked up his cap and started to go out and do what he could to repair the disaster. The imp in his face had fled at the sight of family care. Gaspard had assumed his share of responsibility for this new investment, this costly bit of flesh which made such extravagant demands on the family resources, and this was clearly no time for mischief. But as he reached the door, Puck reappeared for a minute, as he called back: "Say, Mother, why didn't yer get a girl? If boys is ten dollars, you could have got a girl for five, sure!"

XII

WAITING

SHE was waiting for something. You could see it in the anxious lines that puckered incongruously a face that Nature had designed to be as placid as that of a sheep in quiet meadows. She sat heavily in the cheap easy chair with its gaudy covering, but there was no rest in her pose. She bent slightly forward as if she were about to rise at some expected sound. As she knitted busily, every now and then she would turn her head quickly to the window, or she would suddenly stop the click of her needles and listen a moment with her eyes on the door, and then her hands of themselves would resume their work.

The room was a tiny, bare little room, and yet it was evident that her hands had done everything possible to make it look its best. The wooden floor shone from hard scrubbing. The deal table was covered with a home-made patchwork cloth of gay hues. A few photographs and brilliant squares of embroidery or patchwork hung on the walls. On the mantel were some knickknacks made of shell, such as sailors love to bring home, and the photograph of a man. It was the portrait of a common workingman, dressed in his best with a white collar and a new necktie of hues that seemed to impress even the photographic plate. The picture had an irresistible attraction for her, for her eyes kept unconsciously straying toward it, until with a start she would turn again to the window or the door.

It was a strange place in which to expect to find any one living, this tiny room tucked away in the third rear house which a greedy landlord had succeeded in squeezing into the courtyard behind a Cherry Street tenement. The great stream of passers swept by on the street outside, little dreaming that the narrow tunnel beneath that ordinary tenement led into a little world with a population equal to that of a country town. Around the narrow little patch of air that had been left in the process of squeezing, rose four or five tumbledown wooden structures, that seemed to have been thrown together on the impulse of the moment, with no plan save that of utilising every possible inch of space and air. No room was wasted on staircases. The one which ascended to the tiny room was steep as a ladder, partly outside and partly inside the house. Just enough space was allowed overhead for a man of average height to stand upright. A tall man would have had to stoop to get in, and sit down when he entered. One or two rooms at most were all that were allowed to a family, but the rent was only four dollars a month for single rooms and six for double rooms, so that every vacant space was occupied.

The court swarmed with children. Always in the ears of the old woman as she sat and waited sounded the noise of their laughter as they played, or of their cries as some drunken mother cursed them or beat them. By day the court echoed with the shrieks of women as they quarrelled over their clothes lines, and by night with their screams and curses as they fought over their beer. There was dirt everywhere, on faces and clothes and walls and floors. The air was heavy with the odour of it. From every window dirty frowsled heads looked out. Any of these doors might have been opened to reveal a grimy table covered with the remains of a greasy meal, a soiled heap of bedding on the floor, and a broken chair or two.

Hidden away in the midst of these noisy, dirty foreigners, up her narrow little stair in the tiny spotless room, the old woman sat and waited. She would gladly have moved to pleasanter quarters, but for the past two months she had not been able to get even the four dollars necessary for her rent here, and it was only the kindness of the landlady that allowed her even this space. The room was bare enough, but the cupboard was almost empty. A cupful of tea leaves was all that was left; the last scrap of bread had gone the day before. But it was not food for which she was waiting. There was a book open on the table before her, a book that was old and worn. She turned to it once in a while anxiously and read a little, as if she expected some sort of direction or explanation.

Day after day she had sat and waited just as she sat now,— day after day since the morning seven years ago when her husband went away to his work and never came back. No word had ever come from him, and so each day she prepared the room for his return and sat down to wait. She had no friends. She had come to New York as a stranger with her husband. Her acquaintances were limited to the landlady and the grocer and an occasional neighbour who dropped in to borrow a broom or a teapot. At first they had given her a rough sympathy, but after a time they grew impatient with her. " Sure, he's never comin' back. He's dead these five years," they would say. She would look at them sadly as though she did not understand, and would shake her head slowly. Sometimes after several neighbours had spoken in the effort to convince her, she would lose hope. All the expectant light would leave her eyes and her face would grow heavy and sad and dull. Then she would sit again by the gay-covered table and turn the pages of the book in the heaviness of despair. At last her eye would chance upon some promise there, and once more the expectant light would return, and she would start up at the first step on the stair. The neighbours would look at one another and tap their heads and say, "Poor soul."

One day the Lady of Good Cheer found her. She had come in to see the landlady's son who was dying the slow and torturing death of tuberculosis in his little narrow room, and the landlady said: "Ther's a poor soul in the third rear house, and I don't believe she's had a bite to eat these two days. She owes two months, but I haven't had the heart to turn her out."

Very quietly the old woman told the Lady of Good Cheer the story of her waiting. She had grown cautious now, for she had learned to expect criticism when she told her story to the chance acquaintance. But the Lady of Good Cheer found it easy to draw out her secret. The woman had no complaints to offer. It was no "strange mystery," no "terrible fate." If she knew people who would give her sewing then she would not have to go without food, but she had no friends.

"How could I make friends with the like of these?" she said, and nodded her head at a dishevelled woman who was shaking her fist out of the opposite window.

She did not want work that would take her far from home, she said. She wished to be here ready to greet him when he came back.

The Lady of Good Cheer did not try to overthrow her hope or to shake her confidence. This was the woman's whole life, this waiting in unshaken assurance for the return of the man she loved. What were seven years? He had said he would come back. He might be delayed, but he would come. The Lady of Good Cheer said what she could to comfort and cheer, and when she left there was a more peaceful light on the placid face. She sent in a basketful of food, and found sewing enough to provide for the needs of the future. But the one real need she could not satisfy. She could only sympathise. Many a day she would come in and sit down in the little room that was always spotless and ready for his return, and the old woman would push her spectacles up, and they would talk together of his coming.

One day the Lady of Good Cheer knocked and there was no answer. She opened the door. The old woman sat in her easy chair by the gay-covered table, looking toward the door, as she had sat and waited all the seven long and lonely years. But there was no longer on her face the strained and anxious look that told of expectation ever renewed and ever overshadowed by disappointment. There was a look on the placid features that had never been there before — a glad surprise, a complete content and peace. The shouts and screams of the noisy courtyard sounded in through the window, but the old woman would never hear them again. Down below two of the neighbours, who for so many years had mocked at the lonely woman and her absurd delusion, were fighting with shrieks and curses. With the uproar dinning in her ears the Lady of Good Cheer stood in the silence of the little room. From the lips of the dead she could hear something which the heartless cynics outside would never hear or believe: the long waiting had not been in vain. The moment had come that had made up for all the years of loneliness and disappointment. He had come back at last, and had found her at her post, waiting. She had left the little room forever, not in solitude, but in the joy and peace of his return.

XIII

A BATTLE BY NIGHT

It was after ten o'clock Sunday night. The minister and Van Schank were hurrying down Market Street, discussing anxiously the whereabouts and fate of the Lady of Good Cheer. She had been seen to dart off into the darkness after service, and they feared she had ventured into the dangerous and disreputable neighbourhood of Hamilton Street to look up the Summers family, whose absence from church she had noted with dismay. It was a breathless summer's night and the tenement population had crept forth into the streets in the hope of finding precious air. The sidewalk had become a public bedroom; little children slept on blankets on the bare stones, while their mothers, with garments reduced to a minimum, snored in chairs at their side. Each doorstep was a reception room where young matrons gabbled noisily. Here and there, at certain well known corners used by the maidens of the neighbourhood as substitutes for parlours in which to receive their suitors, groups of girls were doing their utmost to attract the young toughs who were making the rounds of the saloons. Now and then could be heard a boisterous laugh, as some rough arm was thrown around a slim waist. The darkness of the street was interrupted by the yellow glare from the flaming torches round the soda booths, which illumined vividly a ring of dark faces and dirty hands that clutched for penny glasses of poisonous looking green or pale pink fluid.

When the minister and Van Schank turned into Hamilton Street after all the noise and glare of the thoroughfare, they seemed suddenly to plunge into blackness and silence. This was no public bedroom and parlour and dining room. The neighbourhood recognised this section as a place entered at night only by those whose purposes were dark. Only a few shadowy female forms followed them stealthily, and here and there a group of men whispered together in the gloom of an alley way. From behind the closed doors of saloons came smothered shouts and curses, and from some of the houses with tight drawn curtains and shut blinds could be heard the sound of laughter and drunken songs. With every step the minister grew more anxious about the Lady of Good Cheer.

"The idea of her coming into a place like this at this time of night," he said. "Why, that crowd would sandbag her merely on the chance of finding a quarter in her purse, and I don't see how she could possibly get through the street without insult."

The two men turned into a narrow tenement

door half way up the street and ran quickly up the four flights of stairs to the top floor. There were four families on each floor as usual, and they knocked at the right hand door on the front. The door opened, and to their great relief there sat the Lady of Good Cheer, talking earnestly with a well-dressed, thick-set man, who was looking at her with a "cat in the cream" expression in his twinkling blue eyes, and a smile of humorous deprecation beneath his yellow moustache. Summers was the kind of man known on the Bowery as a "good jollier." He had an air of confiding frankness that drew one swiftly into intimacy. The twinkle in his eyes and the mischievous quirk about the corner of his mouth were part of the native heritage he had derived from proximity to the Blarney Stone. In spite of his genial and confiding air, however, no one ever succeeded in finding out anything about him. He disappeared from view every day or two, and remained invisible for twelve or fourteen hours. When he returned his pockets were full of bills, but no one, not even his wife, could extort from him any information as to how he got them or where he had been. He turned off every question with an evasive joke, and even those who considered him an intimate friend really knew nothing about him.

The Lady of Good Cheer had met this family through her protégée Mrs. Black, a sister of Mrs. Summers. Mrs. Summers was then "on the street," for although Summers brought in enough money, both he and his wife had been so absorbed in drinking and gambling that their home had been broken up. Mrs. Black had begged the Lady of Good Cheer to do for her sister's husband what she had done for Mr. Black. Summers was disgusted with himself and sad enough over his broken home. He had responded to her appeal with shame-faced frankness and he and his wife had taken the pledge together. The Lady of Good Cheer had started them at housekeeping in this little apartment. The neatness of the room, where every article was fresh and new, bore witness to the success of the experiment and to the efficiency of Mrs. Summers as a housekeeper. Each week some new piece of furniture for the house, or of some article of clothing for the children, was added from the funds Summers brought home. The family had attended church regularly, and this week when they had failed to appear the Lady of Good Cheer was sure that it betokened some disaster, physical or moral, and had hurried to their home heedless of danger to herself in the hope of arriving before the damage was irremediable.

Summers looked up as the minister and his friend entered.

"She's been givin' me a terrible lecture," he said with a rueful smile on his frank face. "Say, you'd orter 'ave heard her," he went on. "She give it to me somethin' fierce, just because I'd been drinkin' a bit and wouldn't lie out of it, like most of your bums."

But the Lady of Good Cheer was in no mood for cajolery. She sat leaning forward, her arms resting on the table and her slender hands clasped lightly, but as she answered him, her eyes were fixed upon Summers with such intensity that his semi-jovial mood began to give way beneath their gaze. Before her passionate appeal in the name of his home and his little ones he could no longer maintain his air of indifference. His eyes dropped and a sheepish look came over his face. As she pleaded with him, she reached out her hand and patted the head of little Mamie, a rosy cherub of two years, who had crept out of bed and was galloping about, her progress impeded by no bodily ornament more serious than her own yellow curls. Lizzie, a thin, sallow child of eight, whose face was prematurely wrinkled by anxiety and pain, was watching the scene from the chair on which she half sat, half stood, her little figure all bent and twisted. Mrs. Summers had been hastily donning her garments in the bedroom, but now her good humoured Irish face appeared at the door. The Lady of Good Cheer ended her appeal by recalling to Summers how, when she first fitted out his home, he had promised that he would start in then and there and live a different life. At this point Summers looked up and ventured a protest.

"Look here," he said. "It ain't no use fer you to talk about me bein' a Christian. I can't be a Christian in my business, and that's straight. It's no use talkin'."

"I should think a man could do right in any business," she said. "If your business is one in which you can't do right, you ought to give it up."

"What! and see my children starve? Not much I oughtn't," he answered.

"Can't you tell me some of your difficulties in your work?" she continued. "Perhaps I could help you."

"Oh, I can't explain it to you," he said evasively, "you couldn't understand!"

His manner discouraged further questions as to his business, and she returned quickly to the main issue. She knew that in spite of his faults he was a man of his word, and her one desire was to get from him a promise that he would drink no more that night. She knew that if he took to the bottle again he would not stop till every penny was gone and all his possessions pawned. But Summers was obdurate.

"I'll promise after I've had another drink," he said.

"Mr. Summers, I can't rest to-night till I have your word," she answered.

"I'm no liar like the rest of these bums, or I'd promise," he said. "But what would be the use of me lyin' to ye. I'm a goin' to have another drink."

Here the minister interfered. "You must go home," he said to the Lady of Good Cheer. "I'll look after Summers."

"I can't leave him till he promises," she said.

Her face was white and haggard, but in spite of physical exhaustion, in her eyes the fire of determination burned bright as ever, and by the set of her firm lips and the tilt of her strong chin a man of less befuddled mind than Summers would have known that he might as well surrender then as later. But with Summers in his present condition the conflict was likely to outlast the night.

"I'll give you my word that Summers won't touch a drop till he sees you in the morning. I'll stay by and see to it," said the minister.

He little knew what he was saying, but she accepted his word unquestioningly. "Very well, then, I'll go," she said. "If you are going to stay, Mrs. Summers and the children had better come with me up to her sister's and spend the night."

They departed in accordance with this arrangement, leaving Summers gazing at the minister and Van Schank in amazed disgust.

"Say, look here! What kind of a holdup is this? You're all right and I'm proud to have ye callin' on me and doin' the social act, but this ain't no time o' night fer kaffy klatches and pink teas," he remarked.

"It is rather late," said the minister, "but you see I promised the Lady of Good Cheer I'd stay until you promised not to drink any more."

"Hully Gee! d'ye think, I'm agoin' ter set the house afire and murder me children on one glass o' beer? I tell ye, I'm agoin' ter have another drink, and then I'll go to bed and to-morrow I'll be sober enough to go to me own funeral."

"It's hard luck, but I'm afraid I'll have to stay till you promise not to drink any more."

"What t'ell! You ain't me grandmother!" said Summers, a sulky look clouding his good-humoured face. "I can swaller me food and drink without no clerical assistance! Me stomach ain't run by no dum syndicate. You mind your business, and I'll mind mine."

"Mr. Summers, this is my business," said the minister. "I'm here for the Lady of Good Cheer. Think what she has done for you. She has cared for you and your family as no mother would have done. She got you this home. She gave you food when you were hungry. She gave clothes to your naked children. All these weeks she has watched over you and planned for you. You know when you drink it is like stabbing her. Don't you suppose that if it would stop you from drinking, she would hold out her hand and let you cut it off?"

At mention of the Lady of Good Cheer, the look of annoyance faded from Summers's face.

"I honestly believe she would, so help me Gawd," he said solemnly.

"Are you going to disappoint a love like that?" said the minister. "You know how she cares. Do you suppose God cares less? She would let her hand be cut off to save you. They really did drive nails through the hands of a man once, and cut his body with the scourge and he allowed it, that you might know how He cares and what He is willing to bear to save you from doing wrong. A true man will not be false to love like that."

"Oh, say now, I tell you it's no use my tryin' to be good in my business. I might as well try to balance an egg on me nose in the middle of a sluggin' match. Them sailors is tough customers to handle. You might wear the knees off yer pants prayin', and there wouldn't none of them budge till you'd loaded him up with booze. And the whole business is crooked. You can't get 'em to hand out their cash ter buy gilt-edged hymn books fer dyin' orphans, and we've gotter get the boodle off 'em somehow. A feller must live."

"How do you do it?" asked the minister, growing interested in the revelation. He had heard something of the runners who went out in row-boats from the sailors' boarding-houses, and met the incoming ships to decoy the sailors to some disreputable place. The business of the runners was to render these men helpless by drugged whisky, and rob them of their pay. Then while still unconscious, the boarding-house keeper would deliver them on board some out-going ship, and receive in return a goodly sum from the captain. Little was known of the situation at the time, for it was before the ring of boarding-house keepers, which controlled all the shipping of sailors in New York, was broken up at great personal risk by the rector of the Floating Church. So effectually was it exposed, however, that the whole iniquitous system, by which the helpless sailors had been defrauded for years, was destroyed.

The note of curiosity in the minister's voice recalled Summers to himself. He glanced keenly at the minister and a mask fell suddenly over his frank countenance.

"Oh, I don't do much!" he said. "I just go out in a boat and jolly the sailors a bit."

He rose to his feet. "Well! I'm off to get another drink, an' then I'm done. I'll drink no more then, not if ye soak me in beer up to me chin."

The minister knew that if he really believed this, his belief was certainly an hallucination. There would be no more stopping after the first drink than after the first yard on a toboggan slide.

"But I promised the Lady of Good Cheer you wouldn't take any at all," he said. "It is very awkward, but I don't see how I can let you go.

You wouldn't have me break a promise to a lady, would you?"

"Now look here!" said Summers, setting his teeth and with an ugly look in his narrowing eyes. "You can promise the Empress of Chiny I won't swaller nothin' but green lemonade and stewed clams, if you like, but I've got to have a drink, all the same, and what's more I'm goin' to get it right now!" and he started forward.

"You'll have to walk right through me then," said the minister, smiling, "for unfortunately I promised to stop you, you know."

"Stop me!" shouted Summers, now thoroughly aroused. "You couldn't do it! not if you was a archangel blowin' on a tin trumpet. Get out o' my way or somethin'll get broke!"

He picked up a heavy club and rushed at the minister. Van Schank jumped to his side in some alarm.

"Thanks! I'll take it on the top of my head and my left ear," said the minister. "Oh, come off, Summers, don't make a fool of yourself. I know you wouldn't hit me."

Summers dropped his stick and looked rather foolish. "You know I'm not here for my own amusement," he went on. "I'm here to help *you*, — your true self, I mean,— for your true self doesn't want to drink. It hates the drink, and I'm here to help you against that devil that is trying to make you do something you know is wrong."

"You're off," said Summers. "Me true self and all the rest of 'em wants a drink, and I'm goin' to get it. If you won't let me out o' the door, I'll jump out the window. I'm desp'rate," and he rushed out on the little balcony that overhung the street, four stories below.

"All right," said the minister, "jump away. Only don't make too bad a spot on the sidewalk." Summers came back from the window with a foolish grin.

"Hear them folks over to the Ink Pot," he said.

"That what?" asked the minister.

"The Ink Pot. That's what they call that joint over in Cherry Street. They're drinkin' and bangin' each other on the head and doin' the fancy song and dance act every night in the year. The can never stops goin' over there, so they calls it the Ink Pot."

The house so designated was an old mansion with colonial doorway and mahogany woodwork, each room of which was now occupied by a large family, and which had become notorious for its noisy altercations. Summers entered upon a racy description of the habits of his neighbours even to the exciting point where they "pulled a gun on the copper." This led to shooting stories, and the minister and Van Schank swapped yarns till the clock struck two.

"Say, I can't stay in here another second. I

Photo by J. H. Denison.

THE INK POT

feel like there was ten cans of dynamite in me each goin' to bust a different way. You sit here and I'll go out and take a walk and come back in a minute," said Summers.

"I'm tired of sitting still myself. I think I'll go along," said the minister.

Summers's face fell. He hesitated a moment. Then he darted to the door.

"I've got to leave you. I'll be back in a second," he said as he slipped out.

"You would better go home and sleep and relieve me in the morning," said the minister to Van Schank.

"All right," he said, "I can hardly keep my eyes open."

The minister did not wait for Summers's return. He hurried downstairs and found him making a bee line for the saloon.

"Hold on a minute," he called. "You came near forgetting me."

"Say, can't you leave a fellow alone long enough to blow his nose?" said Summers with some irritation.

"I would hate to lose sight of a good pal like you," said the minister. "You see, I can't be happy out of your sight."

"You can't wad me ears wid no song and dance like that," said Summers with a rueful grin. "Honest now, I've got ter leave ye. I've got a little business of me own to tend to."

"What's the matter?" asked the minister.

"It's about me wife," he said. "I can't tell you."

"Why, she's fast asleep at her sister's long ago," said the minister.

"Don't you believe it," said Summers, shaking his head in sinister fashion.

"Take my word fer it, you'll never find a woman in the place where she thinks you think she is," he continued darkly. "Whenever she tells you very particular just where she is, you can be dead sure she's somewhere else. It's only when she forgets to tell you where she's goin' that you'll find her there. Oh, she's clever, all right, but she can't fool me. I'm goin' around to her sister's just to prove she ain't there."

"I'm sure she is, and I'll go along and see," said the minister.

Summers ground his teeth in desperation. "Come on, then!" he said, and started up the street like a stone from a catapult.

The streets were still and deserted. Only from the Ink Pot across the way shouts and screams still sounded. There was something awful in the deadly silence of this densely populated street. It seemed as if sudden death had descended on the great city with all its noise and turmoil. Across the way a group of men lurked in the shadow, whispering. Summers stopped and waited for the minister.

"I know that gang," he said. "They're waitin' fer a sailor to come out o' the saloon, well-doped an' leary-eyed, an' they'll give him a jolt with the Black Jack, an' when he comes to, he'll be lucky if he has even a shirt to flap round his ribs."

"Can't we stop them?" asked the minister.

"Not much. It's none of our business. Let 'em alone," and Summers started on. "Say, me nerves is on the bias, an' me veins is skewgeed. I've got to have a rosiner. Wait just a jiff. I'll be back before a skeeter could flip his wing."

But this did not agree with the minister's contract, and so they went through the gamut of argument again, from passionate plea in the name of the holiest to the semi-jocose "jolly." They touched on tears and anger and laughter. Now they were in front of a huge tenement that loomed up vague and shadowy in the darkness.

"Here's the place, now we'll see!" said Summers, and darted through the open door into the long black hallway. It was pitch dark, and they had to grope their way. Strange noises sounded in the darkness before them, heavy breathing and now and then a panting groan. They crept on noiselessly. Suddenly Summers tripped and fell headlong with a curse. A weird cry of terror echoed through the hall and a fearful groan. Two vague figures rose from the ground under the minister's feet, and brushed past, nearly overturning him in the dark. A thrill of horror went through him.

"What's that? Summers! Where are you?" he said.

"The good for nothing bums!" Summers answered in the blackness. "Sleepin' all over the floor, so a decent man can't stir without trippin' over some man's nose, or dirtyin' his shoes in their whiskers. I wisht I had a gun! I'd singe their ears for 'em!"

He crept out the back door into the court and across the court into the rear house, whence soon arose the sound of a violent altercation.

"She's there all right!" said Summers, returning at length. "I pulled her out o' bed to make sure. She done it to fool me. You can't never tell what a woman'll do next. She got on me nerves all right. Say, I'm crazy. I've gotter have a ball!"

"Come, let's walk up to the Bridge," said the minister.

Summers assented sullenly, and once more they made their way through the ghostly streets upon which rested that horror of silence, so intense, so awful, that it was a relief to catch even the sound of a curse from behind the closed doors of a saloon, or to see the skulking figures of the footpads as they awaited their victims.

The first grey light of dawn was breaking when at last they stood on the centre of the great bridge, with its huge piers towering above them, shadowy in the grey light, and the black river swirling far below. Around them in the depths lay the great city, with all its wretchedness and vice and bitter anguish packed into the crowded tenements that stretched away for miles; the great city, with its countless thousands hushed for awhile into insensibility, only too soon to waken to the consciousness of pain and poverty and hunger. The stars paled slowly, and the grey light changed to rose as they leaned on the rails and watched the coming of the dawn.

Still the battle went on. The thirst of Summers seemed to grow with every passing moment to a fire of craving that could not be extinguished. He tried every ruse and every plea that his fertile mind could invent. The minister was conscious only of overpowering weariness. He could scarcely summon energy enough to resist. It was exhausting even to think.

Slowly they walked back. The saloons were beginning to open.

"I've got to have just one ball," said Summers. "I won't be gone a minute."

The minister had not the physical strength for further argument. "All right, go ahead if you must. I'll go in with you," he said, hoping that he could get Summers out after the first glass.

Summers looked at him in solemn disgust.

"D'ye think I could get any soshul enjoyment

swallerin' a glass of whisky wid you standin' there and lookin' at me like that?" he asked. "Sure it would sour on me stummick. I ain't a church-goin' man, but I've got too much respect fer the cloth to be drinkin' in the prisince of a minister."

He turned away from the saloon. "You'll be the death o' me, sure!" he added with a sigh.

Fortunately he took his course past the church. The minister's hope revived. While Summers fixed his eye on a saloon on the opposite corner, he darted to the Church House and pounded on the door. The sexton stuck a towsled head out of the window, and blinked at him in sleepy astonishment. "Get on your clothes and come out here and jolly Summers awhile," he said. "I'm played out."

The sexton grasped the situation and his trousers swiftly and almost simultaneously, and the minister shouted to Summers who was half way across to the saloon: "Oh, Summers! Come here a minute! Dave wants to tell you something!"

Summers returned with a look of despair and disgust on his face. But Dave rose nobly to the emergency. He plunged into a lively discussion of ward politics, and soon had the man's attention. The minister was too exhausted to follow the conversation.

"It is incredible that any human being could want anything so much as that man wants a glass of whisky," he thought as he leaned against the fence. "Why, if one man wanted to reform New York politics and pursued his aim with that same inflexibility of will, the city would be transformed to virtue in a month."

It was seven o'clock at last.

"It's time I went to work," said Summers, looking up as the bells struck. "I'll be off."

"All right," said the minister. "We'll go up and see the Lady of Good Cheer, and then you can go."

"But I'm goin' to have my rosiner," said Summers.

"I don't care about that," said the minister. "I promised you shouldn't drink till you saw the Lady of Good Cheer. After you see her, you can do as you choose."

Summers looked at him with a disgusted grin.

"Well, you are a sticker, for fair!" he said. "Are you through with me after I see her?"

"My responsibility ends then, and I'll bother you no more."

"Come on then, you can't go too quick for me!" said Summers.

They took the car uptown and soon were awaiting the Lady of Good Cheer in the little parlour of her house. She came down fresh and bright, with a happy light in her eyes.

"Oh, Mr. Summers," she cried. "I'm so glad to see you. I knew you would come. You're going to promise me to give up the drink forever, now, aren't you?"

The minister turned aside. He could not bear to be a witness to her disappointment. She had been so sure of this man, and so strong in her faith in him. Now she was to be sadly disillusioned when she saw his purpose, more firmly rooted than ever after a night of deprivation, to drink the moment he left her presence. Then to his utter amazement Summers looked around with a sheepish grin, and said: "All right! here goes. I'll promise."

XIV

THE GLORY IN THE GLOOM

It was one of those sweltering summer days for which New York is famous, but it was not the heat that oppressed the Lady of Good Cheer as she ran up the stairs of a miserable tenement in Hamilton Street. Ordinarily, she was optimistic enough, and even when every one else had lost sight of the star of hope, she still kept the vision of a last, lingering gleam. But she had come upon many terrible scenes behind the walls of these tenements, and to-day she had the uncomfortable sense that some hideous discovery awaited her on the other side of the closed door on the third floor front, and she shuddered slightly as she knocked upon it.

It was not a very pleasing voice that invited her to come in, nor was it an especially attractive apartment into which she entered. The table had not been cleared from the recent meal, which, she judged by the appearance of the children who greeted her, had been taken externally as well as internally. A dish or two of soup had been upset upon the table and was trickling down to the floor, which was in its turn littered with a debris of bits of food and rags in the middle, and in the corners some greasy blankets and dirty comforters on which the children had slept. Everywhere were the evidences of a simple life with no attempt at division of labour or classification of function, but with all the utensils of eating, sleeping, clothing and washing mingled in a promiscuous disarray on furniture and floor. Mrs. Black, the lady of the house, was barefooted, her ragged dress was open at the throat, and her tangled hair was tumbling down her back. The corners of her mouth drooped, and her eyes were red and watery, a modern Niobe, by whose side her ancient prototype seemed almost cheerful. One child, whose face was smudged by soup and dirt, clung to her skirts and howled, and the sick baby in her arms moaned and sobbed. The two other children were rolling on the floor and pummeling each other, somewhat to the alarm of the cockroaches that had been feeding on the crumbs and were now scuttling away to their favourite retreat behind the picture on the wall.

The Lady of Good Cheer stood in the midst of this chaos, reflecting that the condition of the room seemed to call for critical comment. But she knew that cleanliness is an expensive matter where one is called upon to take continual care of a sick baby and three ailing children, and to do the cooking and washing at the same time, and she realised that Mrs. Black had no income for luxuries. Besides, she had no attention to give to superficial issues just now, for she feared that this little home, in which she had been interested for many months, was threatened with overwhelming disaster.

During the last winter, in the course of her rounds, the Lady of Good Cheer had entered one of those unique and far-famed hostelries which at present occupy some of the old houses adjoining the Cherry Street mansion once occupied by General Washington. They do not presume to offer guests a room or even a bed. Lodgings are rented at the rate of five cents a spot, the spot including a heap of rags that have been accumulating more odour than sanctity from Revolutionary days, and also a can of frothy substance known as mixed ale, the mixture being a minimum of ale and a maximum of old rinsings. To this hospitable place there repaired nightly some twenty or thirty ancient hags, ragged, maudlin with drink, and in general well equipped to play extempore the part of Macbeth's witches. They were busied in selecting their spots and among their grotesquely repulsive faces, the Lady of Good Cheer noted one which by contrast seemed quite angelic. Its owner was young, at least, and sober and reasonably clean. The Lady of Good Cheer inquired her reasons for sleeping in such a loathsome place, and she burst into tears, and told the old story of a home broken up because a man had too little to do and too much to drink.

The Lady of Good Cheer was interested in her new find, and promptly hunted up the husband to see if there was in him the timber from which a home might be built. With his smooth cheek and beardless chin and soft brown eyes, he seemed an amazingly boyish creature to have the responsibility of a wife and four children, but she liked his clear-cut profile and quick, deft movements, and soon discovered that his hands were unusually clever, and that the muscles of his lithe body were like iron. He had been ruined by his very cleverness. He was handy at every trade, and had never learned any thoroughly. The man who "can do anything" is only employed where men are willing to take anybody. This year with thousands of skilled workmen idle, no one seemed to need the services of Black. He was frank enough to admit, however, that in his case there were other causes of disaster. He stated plainly that "drink was his curse," and so serious a curse that no charm had proved adequate to remove it. He explained that he had taken the pledge from the priest, but it "had not worked." It was evidently the fault of the priest or of the pledge. His conversation with the Lady of Good Cheer gave him hopes that a pledge administered by her might prove more potent. Religion was a science as unfamiliar to him as calculus, but he was convinced that without its assistance a pledge was an absurdity. So he knelt with her and in words whose earnestness and sincerity made up for their theological ambiguity, sought the power to keep his promise.

When this preliminary step had been achieved, the Lady of Good Cheer found rooms for him in Hamilton Street. The neighbourhood was not choice in this most disreputable street in the ward, but she selected the rooms not for their social prestige or external charm, but because the rent was but $7.50 a month. She furnished them with the rudimental equipment for housekeeping, and the Blacks and their four children moved in. The best she could do in the way of work was to secure for Black the chance to clean up a down-town office every morning at a wage of $2.50 a week, and, starting with this, he had made a most heroic effort to maintain his home. But to support a family on $2.50 a week and pay a rent of $7.50 a month requires more necromancy than heroism. Black tried every means and exhausted every expedient. He would hang around the market and pick up here and there a fish that had been repudiated by the dealers, and carry it home in triumph to satisfy the little mouths that were always clamouring for food. He tramped the streets in every unoccupied hour, looking for a chance to earn a few pennies to buy bread. But there was never enough, and each day he came back to face the reproaches of his pale wife and listen to the laments of his little ones, who were always hungry and ailing. It was a hard enough trial of faith for a church warden to behave with becoming self-control in that breathless sweltering heat, and for a man goaded by despair and unreasonable reproaches, and maddened by an unsatisfied appetite, it required a self-denying fortitude little short of the miraculous to return on pay-day, past the long row of saloons with the odour of alcohol heavy in the air, and bring back untouched every penny of his earnings. Like some sensitive instrument, the Lady of Good Cheer had felt the steadily increasing tension. To-day was his pay-day, and she knew it would be a crisis in his life. There was for him no middle ground. One glass meant madness and utter ruin.

These were the reasons that as soon as she was free that afternoon she had hurried as swiftly as her feet would carry her to the tenement in Hamilton Street. Now she was searching Mrs. Black's face in the hope of being assured that her dark anticipations had been unfounded. But Mrs. Black was never what could be called a cheerful or animated person. On her happiest days she stood with slouching shoulders and watery eyes and a deprecatory smile on her drooping mouth, and her attitude was as depressing to the observer as the sight of a rain-drenched cypress in a bog. To-day she overflowed with tragedy. There seems to exist among the poorest the consciousness that for them the only chance of playing an heroic or important part in the eyes of the world lies in some desperate calamity or crime, and Mrs. Black was uplifted by the sense that she was the heroine of an important drama. In this rôle of leading lady her face lost its expression of weary discouragement and acquired a tragic animation. She wasted no breath in greetings, but plunged at once to the crisis.

"He's gone back to the drink!" she cried. "I always knew he would! I've been a tellin' him so every day since he swore off! To-day he got that mad at me fer sayin' it, that he run off and drank to get the nerve to answer me back. That's the talk he gives me. An' he comes back and tells me I'm a liar and he'll prove it. An' when I tells him, what else could I expect from him wid a low-down drinkin' mother, and no one knowin' his father, he ups and calls me all the names — you never heard such langwidges! He was somethin' fierce! Such a row he made the neighbours all come runnin' in, and then off he goes like a crazy man. I was scared o' me life, and I run up stairs to me sister, Mrs. Summers, on the top floor. Well, sure enough, after gettin' a drink or two, back he comes. I'd locked the door o' me house, and I hears him a poundin' and a cursin' and me sister calls out to him from the entry above to stop his noise. Wid that he begins to call her all the names, shoutin' so all the neighbours could hear. An' me pore old mither — sure he said she was nothin' but a dirty old — savin' your prisince, I'd niver be tellin' you the words what he said. An' me sister, she tells him mighty plain who was his father and his grandmother and all the rest of his family. An' wid that he comes a rushin' up the stairs, an' me sister who'd been washin' and was standin' over her tubs in the entry,— I'll not be sayin' she hadn't been drinkin' a bit too,— she yells: 'Sure he's comin' to murdher us!' and she picks up a tub full o' water wid both hands and gives it a heave over the balusters right on top of him. You should 'ave heard the row! The tub lit on his hand, and smashed up two of his fingers, and the soap-suds covered him wid lather till he looked like the wild man o' Borneo. I never see such a lookin' thing in all me life. An' yell! — say ye could 'ave heard him clean to the Battery! The neighbours caught him and shoved him down stairs, and him swearin' he'd buy a pistol and come back and shoot us all!"

This was the drama, rehearsed with many shakes of the head and cluckings of the tongue. It was a sad ending, this hideous drunken brawl, to all the plans the Lady of Good Cheer had made. Yet after all she could not help feeling a bit proud of Black after all. Six months of starvation and dubious fish, combined with a complaining wife and four ailing children, is a stern test for any hero. Even a Siegfried might have failed to meet it. At any rate he had not disappointed his wife, whose self-satisfaction in being able to say, "I told you so," seemed undimmed by any consciousness that it was she who had driven him back to "the drink." The Lady of Good Cheer could only regret that her influence had not been constant enough to counteract this unfailing stimulus of pessimistic suggestion. There was nothing to be done now but to stand up and try to repair the damage. She provided that the terror-stricken wife should take refuge with Mrs. Kiley, another sister who lived two blocks away in Monroe Street, and went home to spend an anxious night.

Black, however, felt no need of assistance or pity. The alcohol burnt in his brain like a flame. He was no longer a helpless, ragged wretch, kicked out of offices when he asked for work, and sneaking around the markets to pick up refuse. He was a giant; he could handle an army of policemen with one hand! Moreover, he had a great vocation: to purge the world of a false woman whom he had once thought the most charming and fascinating of creatures. He, too, was impressed by dramatic possibilities. Here was a thing to be played in the Windsor Theatre upon the Bowery. He drew his money and bought a pistol. He loaded the pistol, and sought his house, his head up, his plans made. Now he had power; now he could defy the world! He crept stealthily up the steps of his house, and with superb dramatic effect flung open the door of his room and shouted: "Prepare to meet thy God!" He had seen the words hung as a motto in Dennett's ten-cent restaurant underneath a sign, "Mince pie, five cents."

The association with the pie had not seemed significant to him and the words struck him as impressive and appropriate. But there was no answer. The room was empty. He waited sometime for his wife's return, planning out a dramatic crisis that would astonish the world when reported in *The Journal.* Then when it grew late and Mrs. Black still did not appear, he thought of Mrs. Kiley's house, and to Mrs. Kiley's house he hurried, his exaltation increasing as the end drew near.

Mrs. Kiley lived in a rear house on the ground floor. Black entered the house in front, and passed through the hall to the court behind. Should he call her out, he wondered, and shoot her without warning? No, she must have time to reflect on her sins, and to realise that her doom had come at last at the hands of an innocent and avenging husband. He looked out through the door into the court upon which Mrs. Kiley's windows opened. There in the open window sat Mrs. Black, dishevelled and ragged as usual. Now was his chance! He stepped forth imitating as well as he could the voice of the hero at the Windsor Theatre, he shouted: "Are you ready to die?" and pointed his pistol directly at her. The effect equalled his most ardent expectations. Mrs. Black turned and saw the pistol. Her sallow face turned pasty white, and shriek after shriek filled the court. Mrs. Kiley screamed. The neighbours came rushing out, but before any of them could move, there was a loud, sharp report, and Mrs. Black sank to the floor with a groan. The screams redoubled, and from a dozen doors men rushed out upon the avenging husband.

In a moment it appeared that Mrs. Black was only frightened. The bullet had passed over her head and had struck into the wall. As the men rushed toward him to seize him, Black stood looking at them calmly and contemptuously. Didn't they know that he could destroy the whole world with one hand? He would show them. At the sight of the smoking pistol in his hand, they grew cautious. One of them slipped out and called a policeman, and while Black faced the men from the house, the policeman slipped up behind and wrenched the pistol from his hand. Black turned on him with such sudden ferocity that the officer went down with a crash. He rapped on the pavement and in a moment two more officers appeared. A fit of madness was upon Black. What were policemen? — he could brush them away like flies! As he fell upon them, his slight wiry body seemed charged by electric force. His arms flew like the spokes of a driving wheel. The policemen felt as though a cyclone had struck them, and went down like ninepins before they knew what had happened. They drew their clubs and attacked him, but he was insensible to pain. He made no effort to defend himself as their blows fell on his head and shoulders. He fought with fists and elbows, with knees and feet, with head and teeth, and in every movement he was as quick as an infuriated wild cat. The battle went on witnessed by a gathering crowd, and it was not until two more policemen came up that they mastered him and carried him off writhing, twisting, biting, like a captured tiger, while they showered blows on his head.

The next day the Lady of Good Cheer visited Black in the Ludlow Street jail. Through the minister she had interviewed the magistrate, and told him the story of Black's struggle. Mrs. Black was well terrified, but she agreed not to press the charge if her husband could be kept away from her. The magistrate thought that he might be willing to suspend sentence, if the Lady of Good Cheer and the minister would agree to be responsible for Black. She entered the gloomy building, with its three tiers of cells built up within the enclosing walls and reached only by little iron fire-escapes. She climbed the narrow iron stairs accompanied by an officer, passed along the iron gallery, and stood at last in front of a grating behind which Black was confined. She peered through the bars of the iron cage, and there in the darkness of the narrow cell, seated on the pallet on one side, she saw a form crouched and bent, with head sunk low. "Mr. Black!" she called. The head lifted, and she saw not a face, but a shapeless mass of bruises, blackened, swollen eyes, a disfigured nose, cut lips and a head whose numerous gashes had soaked with blood the white bandage that swathed it. He looked up at her in a dazed way. The exaltation and madness was gone. His great battle with the social order was over, and once more he was only a poverty-stricken wretch, friendless and helpless in the clutch of that iron monster, Law. He knew that he had incurred a penalty of seven years in jail.

"Looks pretty bad," said the officer. "Pounded his head against the iron bars like a crazy man last night."

The Lady of Good Cheer thought it more probable that his wounds were the result of the usual punishment inflicted for resistance, but she said nothing. She spoke quietly with Black of his escapade and her disappointment, but he only looked at her dully.

At last she said: "If I can get the judge to let you off, will you promise to do just what I say?"

A sudden flash of light came into his eyes.

"Can ye get me off. Oh, can ye get me out o' this," he cried in a low frightened voice. "Fer God's sake get me out if ye can!"

"Will you promise never to touch the drink, and to live on the West Side, and never to see your wife?" she asked.

"Sure I will,— I'll promise anything. Oh, fer God's sake, help me out of this!"

"Remember if you touch a drop of liquor or

are seen with your wife, even a moment, you are liable to be sent back to jail on the instant."

"I won't never break my promise, so help me God," he muttered.

Then while curious faces were peering through the gratings of the neighbouring cells, he repeated after her the solemn promise to take up again the dreary struggle for existence that he had just abandoned to play his part in the drama of his disastrous battle with the social order. The magistrate was inclined to think that when his fears wore off, he would return to his evil habits, but when Black appeared before him, he delivered to him a fatherly lecture on his misdemeanour. Black was dismissed under suspended sentence, and he went out bewildered, hardly able to realise his good fortune. He had seen himself surrounded by those iron walls for seven long years and now here he was, a free man, jostled by the swarming Jews of Grand Street.

The Lady of Good Cheer found rooms for him on the West Side, and before long secured work which brought him better pay. It seemed like a modern miracle, but Black kept his word.

A month or so later the Lady of Good Cheer was walking home from an evening meeting. It was a glorious moonlight night, and after the intense heat of the day, the people of the tenements were enjoying it to the full. Sidewalks were filled with laughing couples, and doorsteps were crowded with loosely clad housewives gossiping with their neighbours. On a step just at the corner sat a young couple; so absorbed in one another that they caught the attention of the Lady of Good Cheer. How could there be romance in lives such as theirs, she wondered, or any possibility of escape from the dull facts of poverty and hunger and ceaseless toil? The man's arm stole around the woman and he drew her gently toward him. As the woman moved, the moon shone full upon her face, and the Lady of Good Cheer was astonished to recognise the drooping mouth and pale cheeks of Mrs. Black. But the watery eyes seemed to shine with an unaccustomed light, and her face in the moonlight looked almost pretty. The Lady of Good Cheer took a step forward, and saw the face of the man beside her. She knew the clear cut features and keen eyes in a moment. It was Black himself.

The thought of rebuking Black never once entered the mind of the Lady of Good Cheer. She did not send him back to jail. She went quietly on her way, with a sort of exultation in her heart, to know that even in the midst of degradation and hunger, hatred and murder, the love of a man for his wife is a thing strong enough and beautiful enough to conquer fear and hate and the dread of weary toil, and to cover them over with the mystic glory of romance.

Not long after, a pleasant set of rooms in a

street near by was secured, and Black and his family were established to start again the great struggle together, this time with better chance of success. And until the strength of the brave man yielded at last to the dread disease that haunts the tenements, that home continued to be a joy to the Lady of Good Cheer.

XV

THE BRIGHT SIDE

"To be blind is to see the bright side of life."
— HELEN KELLER.

THE Lady of Good Cheer was conducting the minister and a group of singers from the church on one of their Sunday afternoon tours. The house they entered was a queer old edifice, built of brick and standing on a prominent corner, but its sadly dilapidated walls had given up all pretensions to the pride of life. The Lady of Good Cheer ran lightly up the ancient staircase, on which chaos had left its marks, and soon her slender form disappeared in the dark attic hall. The others groped their way after her and presently found themselves in a large gloomy front room. The shutters were closed and the windows shut, and the air was heavy with the odour of unwashed clothes and rags and greasy garments. A shrill barking greeted the visitors, and a miserable little black terrier rushed out and began excitedly to worry their ankles.

The minister threw open the shutters, and the light shone in upon an aged woman sitting crouched in a huge broken armchair. On the face of the woman was the strained, anxious look characteristic of the blind, and she turned her sightless eyes from side to side, as though following the unwonted steps and commotion in her silent chamber. She tried to struggle to her feet to meet her guests, but the Lady of Good Cheer was at her side with a greeting of sympathy, and bade her keep her seat. At the sound of her visitor's voice, a light came into the sightless face. She seemed to see the Lady of Good Cheer in each tone and inflection, as others saw her soul in the high brow and aquiline nose, and in the firm lips and deep set eyes. For her voice was one of those that seems to thrill with a thousand familiar associations,— a voice that one has heard from earliest childhood, so soft in sympathy and so firm in command.

"Is your son here?" the Lady of Good Cheer asked. She had just equipped the old woman's son with a new outfit of wearing apparel, complete even to necktie and collar.

"He's not here, but he promised to come," said the old woman. "He's a good boy to me. He's all I have. I don't know what I should do without him. He takes care of me, and cooks for me, and keeps the house clean. I can't do nothing now but sit still. It's a hard thing to be blind," she added with a sigh and then her face brightening, "But there ain't many that have a boy like mine to take care of them."

The Lady of Good Cheer looked around the

room. It did not look as if it had been cleaned in years. A dirty comforter or two lay where they had been thrown in the corners. The floor was littered with soiled rags and broken crockery and bones. The wretched little terrier who was never taken out had added to the unspeakable filth of the place. The furniture had once been handsome, but the upholstery was soiled and torn and the curtains ragged.

"Yes, he's a good boy," the old woman went on. "I never could live here if he didn't clean it up and look out for everything for me."

"Didn't you own this house once?" asked the Lady of Good Cheer.

"Yes," said the old lady. "I had plenty of money then, and owned this house and the one over the way, but my boy is unlucky. He's good to his mother, but he's very unlucky, and somehow all the money's gone now, and we had to sell the house and move to the attic here. But I kept all my best furniture, and you see I'm quite fine up here." And the sightless eyes travelled proudly around the room over the furniture and curtains and pictures, that in her sight still retained their former elegance.

Just then there was an uncertain step in the hall and the door opened and the "boy" entered. The Lady of Good Cheer looked at him aghast. He was a man of about 30, clad in ragged trousers that a torn belt confined with some uncertainty about the waist, a rusty cutaway coat, soiled and torn, and a dirty yellow shirt that had no collar and was open at the throat. His face was unshaven, and his hair unbrushed. He hung his head, and looked about with shifty eyes.

"Is it my boy?" said the old woman, her voice thrilling with pride and joy. "I'm so glad he's come. I want you to know my boy," she said to the minister. "There aren't many poor blind mothers as have so fine a boy to look after them and take care of them. I can't thank God enough for what he's left me when he took away my sight," and a tear stole from the sightless eyes and trickled down the furrowed cheek. "But where are the clothes?" said the Lady of Good Cheer to him. "I lost 'em. I had bad luck," said the "boy," *sotto voce* and looking at her with his shifty eyes. As he spoke, they noticed that his breath reeked with vile alcohol. The mother caught the last words. "Yes, poor boy, he always has bad luck. I don't know why the world is so hard on him. Seems as if God was against him."

They had come to hold a little meeting at the old lady's request. They found seats on the ragged furniture, and sang the old songs she wanted to hear and read some comforting words. Then came the prayer, and each looked anxiously about for an available spot on that unspeakably dirty floor, where they might kneel without permanent damage to their garments. They finished the meeting successfully, though the terrier was the cause of some incoherence in the petitions when he jumped suddenly upon the minister's back as he knelt in prayer, much to the delight of the more unregenerate youth in the party, as they peered between their fingers to discover the cause of the hiatus in the minister's ideas, and discovered his desperate efforts to dislodge the little beast. Even the Lady of Good Cheer could not keep her eyes fast closed during the distracting scene, and the sightless eyes of the old lady were the only ones that saw nothing to mar the solemnity of the little service. When they had finished she thanked them for their prayers with tears in her eyes, saying that it was many, many years since she had been to church.

"And I have so much to thank God for, I know I ought to go," she added. "You see my money's all gone now, and if I hadn't a boy who would take care of his old mother and bring her in something to eat, it would go hard with me."

"Did you get that jelly, I sent you?" asked the Lady of Good Cheer, casually.

"Yes," said the old lady. "I've got some of it still."

"That isn't much of a recommendation for it," said the Lady of Good Cheer, her eyes twinkling. "I'm afraid it didn't taste very good."

"Oh, it is delicious," said the old lady. "I never tasted anything so good. I don't want to use it up, so I take a teaspoonful and put it in a cup of hot water." She interrupted herself. "You see my son has been very unlucky lately and I haven't had any tea, but the jelly and water was even better than tea."

"What did you have to eat with it?" asked the Lady of Good Cheer.

"Oh, my boy always brings me a bit of bread, that is almost always, except when he's very unlucky. Yes, God is very good to me, and I hope you'll thank the lady that sent that jelly, and tell her I enjoyed it a whole month."

They said good-bye and started down the dark stairs. "I believe the poor old soul has lived on that jelly and water the past three weeks," said the Lady of Good Cheer. "I had no idea she was in want of food. She is always so cheerful and never complains. I shall send her in a good meal right away."

"Who will cook it?" asked the minister.

"I'll run in and cook it myself," she answered. "I would not trust it to that son. He would sell it or pawn it, as he did his clothes. And if he didn't, think of eating anything that he cooked!" and she shuddered. "I took the oculist to see her this week," she went on, "but he says there is no hope. She can never regain her sight." And the minister murmured involuntarily, "Thank God."

XVI

A MAN WITH FIVE LIVES

"WON'T ye come down ter my house and talk wid me husband? Sure he's goin' on like a crazy man and I'm scared o' me life."

Mrs. Ferguson stood at the church house door, where she had just caught the Lady of Good Cheer as she was sallying forth to her work. As she spoke she tried to hide her disordered hair beneath the grey shawl in which her dumpy figure was wrapped. Her stout round face was disturbed from its customary placidity, and her narrow, pale eyes, peeping out above fat bulging cheeks, surveyed the Lady of Good Cheer anxiously.

"There's no one he'll listen to but you and the minister, and he's like to kill himself now," she went on.

"Of course I'll come," said the Lady of Good Cheer.

She stopped to leave word for the minister and the nurse to follow her, and then hurried down the street, toward the river, through crowds of barefoot, ragged children and Jewish merchants. Mrs. Ferguson lived on the top floor of a miserable tenement in Water Street, opposite some great warehouses and factories.

As she and the Lady of Good Cheer made their way up the dark, narrow stairs, and drew near the room, they heard muttered curses, then a shout and a heavy thud. They threw open the door of a bare room, scantily furnished with a bed, a table, a stove and a few chairs. In the middle of the room stood a heavily built man of medium height dressed in the soiled blue jumper and belted trousers commonly worn by teamsters. He was muttering to himself, and as they entered, he turned suddenly and struck a furious blow behind him.

"There! you cursed Dago! I gave you one that time! What do you mean, you robbers, creeping around behind me like that? You can't stick no knife in *my* back. I'll show you if you can," and he made a furious rush across the room striking madly with both arms.

His heavy-featured face was distorted, his pale blue eyes rolled wildly under bushy brows, and his lips moved convulsively beneath his thick brown moustache.

"You see, he's got the D. T.'s bad," said Mrs. Ferguson in a whisper.

The Lady of Good Cheer took a step forward. She looked unusually trim and slight in her close-fitting suit of dark blue. She held her head high, and her lips were straight and determined, though she spoke lightly, as if in casual friendly greeting.

"Good morning, Mr. Ferguson," she said. "I am glad I found you at home this morning. I haven't had a chance to see you in a long time."

The man paused, turned and faced her. He passed his hand over his eyes and brushed back the tangled hair from his brow. The wild expression faded from his face, and he looked at her with a quiet, benevolent smile, and spoke in his usual slow, gentle manner.

"Why how d'ye do, ma'am, I didn't see you was here. I'm glad to see you. Come in and sit down."

"I see you're off from work to-day," she went on as she took a seat, watching him closely with her deep-set eyes, as if she was trying to hold him with their gaze.

He returned her look with a pleased frankness. "Yes, I took a day off. I wanted a rest." A sudden expression of fear came into his eyes, and he looked furtively to the corner where the bed stood. "But these cursed Dagos give me no peace. They follow me everywhere," he said savagely.

"I don't see them now," she said quietly. "I think they must have gone away."

He gave a sudden shout. "Look! there's one under my bed," and he rushed furiously across the room.

The Lady of Good Cheer stepped swiftly to his

side, and put her hand on his shoulder as he stooped to look under the bed.

"Come and sit down," she said. "I'll watch and see that no one will hurt you. I can warn you if any one is creeping up behind. Never mind the man under the bed. He can't do any harm."

Ferguson went back meekly and took his seat. The madness had faded from his eyes and he was placid again.

"I don't seem to see them any more now you're here," he said. "I guess you scared them away." He gave a sigh of relief. "I'm glad they've gone. They've been trying to murder me all day. I've had lots of narrow escapes in my time, and I'd hate to be done up by a rascally Dago."

"What escapes have you had?" asked the Lady of Good Cheer, hoping to keep his attention until the hallucinations should be dissipated.

"Well," he said, "it's a queer thing for sure, but I've been killed, as you might say, four times already. The first time, I was workin' in a grain elevator. They was hoistin' the grain up in a lift, and I was up at the top of the shaft to unload it. You know how tall them grain elevators is, taller'n a six-story tenement. Well, I went to the edge of the shaft to look over and see if the car at the bottom wasn't pretty near loaded. I was hangin' over the edge and lookin' way down in the dark at the men piling oats on the car, when of a sudden, one foot slipped on a pile of oats on the edge. I made a grab to save meself, but it was too late. Down I went into the dark old shaft. Well, say, now! It was a great fall for sure! I thought I was a dead man, of course. Seems like I thought over all me sins and everythin' I ever done, while I was a fallin' down that there dark hole. And all the while the floor was comin' nearer, and I was thinkin', 'In a minute now, there's an end of you,' and then I struck, and thinks I, 'Now, I'm dead.' Well, it was all dark, and I thought I must be buried deep in the earth. I could feel it all around me, in me mouth and in me eyes. And I began to try to get it out of me mouth. And then I found that me hands were stretched up above me head, and I couldn't get them down. And while I was suffocatin' and tryin' to breathe, I felt somethin' catch hold of me hands and it pulled and pulled, and the next minute up I come, and there I was sittin' in the oats in the car at the bottom of the shaft. I went in feet first — clean over me head and over me hands that were stretched up. And they dug in and found me hands, and pulled me out. I was near smothered, but I wasn't hurt, not even a little bit."

The Lady of Good Cheer expressed her amazement at this astonishing escape, and seeing his eyes begin to wander anxiously toward the bed, she asked: "You say there were other escapes. Tell me the next one."

"Well," he said, "that was some years later.

I was livin' in a tenement down in New Chambers Street, next the coal-yard there. It was a terrible hot summer, and we uster go up on the roof in the afternoon to get cooled off. There wasn't no railing to the roof, and it sloped down to the edge, so the old woman, she didn't like it much, and she'd sit away up in the middle where it was hot. But I found a spot down near the edge behind a chimbley where it was cool. One afternoon, I got home from work early and went up on the roof to sit, while the old woman was getting the supper. There was two or three women settin' around up there, and I went down to my chimbley and lay down, and in a minute I was fast asleep. Well, I must have had a bad dream and jumped, fer the next thing I knew I was just rollin' off the edge of the roof. I gave a yell like an Indian, and grabbed at the eaves, but it was no go. The women on the roof screeched and yelled, 'Fire! Fire!' at the top of their voices, but it didn't stop me. Down I went through the air, five stories down! Say, but I was scared! I thought, 'This time I'm dead for sure! Down I come with a bang, and then all was dark. Well, the next thing I knew, I felt some one pourin' water over me, and there I was sittin' on a great pile of this black coal dust in the coal yard, with a lot of firemen around squirting me with a hose. Some one heard the women cry, 'Fire!' and turned in an alarm. The firemen came rushing around, and some one told them I'd just fell off the roof. So they sees there was a big hole in the pile of fine coal next the tenement, and they digs me out and washes me off with a hose. I was a sight to make ye scream, but it never hurt me a bit. I walked up and ate my supper just the same as ever."

The Lady of Good Cheer ventured to imply that there might be some inaccuracy of detail in this story.

"No, I'm givin' it to ye straight. Sure as I stand here, it happened just like I'm tellin' ye. You can ask me wife."

"You certainly didn't have any more such adventures?" she asked.

"Sure, I did," said Ferguson. "The next happened two years after when I was workin' wid the city. They put me on one of the scows that carries the sewage down the harbour. I had to make the trip every day, an' I never liked the job much. The old scow had a mast and boom, so as they could rig up a sail when the wind was right to help the tug along. Well, one day the water was rough, and the old scow was bouncin' and sloppin' along and I was settin' in the stern pretendin' to steer her. But I got kinder sleepy with the rockin' of the boat, and the next thing I knew, she gave a terrible big rock and the boom swung clean over and caught me right side o' the head, and over I went, kersplash! I never could swim, and if I could, it wouldn't have done me no good, I was that stunted. But the man on the tug was a spry young feller. I don't understand to this day how he done it, but he managed to swing the tug around, and he caught me with a hook just as I was goin' down the last time. That was a terrible close call, and it took him an age to get the water out of me and the breath into me again.

"I took to the shore after that and got onto the Street Cleaning Department. I went around with a cart, and had to empty them big cans of garbage along the street. I had to lift the can — it was mighty heavy, you can bet — and climb up on the hub, and empty it into the cart. Well, one day it had been snowin' and freezin', and things was slippery. I caught up a monstrous heavy can, and climbs up on the hub with it to empty it. Just as I gets it up above me head, me foot slips off the hub, and down I comes with the can on top o' me. Well, what happened, I don't rightly know. They said me head was caught between the hub and the can. Anyway, me head was all broken and splintered. They carried me up to the hospital, and cut out all the broken bone and splinters and put in a silver top to me skull. You can see the scar on the top o' me head," he said, pushing aside his tangled hair, and showing a huge bare scar in the midst of it. "I suppose, that's the reason I gets so queer these hot days. It heats up the silver and I gets kind o' light headed. I'm a Democrat, ye know, and the boys are always jollyin' me about free silver, and silver on the brain. I think that's the reason I can't drink. The drink must do something to that silver plate, and it sets me pretty nigh crazy."

"I asked the nurse to bring down some medicine for you," said the Lady of Good Cheer. "You'll take it, won't you, when she brings it?"

"Oh! I be glad to get anything to stop me headaches. They're somethin' fierce."

He was talking naturally now, and seemed free from hallucination, and when the nurse arrived with the medicine, the Lady of Good Cheer was able to assure him that all danger was over for the present.

It was some months later that Mrs. Ferguson came to her again. She was in tears, and even more agitated than before.

"Me husband didn't come home last night, an' I can't find him nowheres. He ain't been down to his work, an' the police don't know nothin' about him. Don't seem as if nothin' could have happened to him. He's so lucky, he always seems to get out of every scrape. But I'm terrible anxious. What can have come over him?"

The Lady of Good Cheer did her best to console her. For three days they ransacked the city, but they found no trace of him. On the third day of the search some workmen, who were working at a dump, under a wharf, found a strange shape floating in the dark water. They pulled it ashore, and though the features were unrecognisable, the clothing was soon identified as that of Mr. Ferguson. He had entered the gates of death for the fifth time, and this time he had not returned.

XVII

A MODERN MIRACLE

HAMILTON STREET was not a spot where one would look for marvels of saintliness. The miracles that seemed appropriate to that dismal alley were such as might emanate from the direct intervention of the powers of darkness that seemed irresistibly entrenched behind the long line of dirty and battered tenements and ancient decaying dwelling houses. Behind the walls that fronted the streets was a second line of fortification, a row of squalid rear houses, some of which were mere tumble-down sheds, others huge crowded hives, swarming with strange life. These were invisible from the street, and could only be approached through dark tunnels beneath the front houses, each of which led into a narrow, dirty court full of refuse and children, cats and babies and drunken sailors.

As the Lady of Good Cheer passed down the narrow dark street, she could not shake off the sense that a malevolent foe was watching like some huge octopus with baleful gaze from behind the close shuttered windows of the disreputable houses, ready to reach out a slimy, tentacled arm through the swinging side door of some dive and clutch its victim. This feeling was not without grounds. Here was the spot where a few days before, a man had been sandbagged; there at the corner she had seen a sailor knocked down and robbed; here on this door step one of the young toughs had been shot but a few days since by the leader of a rival set.

Each saloon was the headquarters of a gang which lay in wait for hapless sailors. Only a few days since the minister had met a crowd of them convoying an intoxicated sailor and going through his pockets at the same time. They had administered knockout drops to him, as he was too vigorous an old salt for them to handle while he was in fighting trim, and just as they met the minister the sailor fell unconscious on the pavement. The minister requisitioned an empty push cart, dumped the senseless man into it, and wheeled him away from his would-be plunderers, to the church, where he soon came to himself and irritated by his unexpected change of environment, proceeded to curse the priests and all clergy with a most varied and vivid vocabulary.

This was Hamilton Street. One would certainly not search for moral strength in a dirty rear tenement behind one of these saloons, or for spiritual uplift in the presence of an ignorant and corpulent Irishwoman who had been brought up among brawls and street fights, to know no other inspiration than that of the beer can. Yet it was to such a spot that the Lady of Good Cheer liked to turn when her work had been especially discouraging, and she never failed to go away with a sense that here was more real evidence of the force that lies behind religion than she had ever discovered in any cathedral, no matter how impressive the service.

She passed on down the street in front of windows with broken panes whence hideous old hags leered at her, past a "Black and Tan Dive," which had just been raided by the police, and turned in at last at the side door of one of the saloons. She entered a dark narrow tunnel leading under the building, and came out into a tiny court in the rear. Huge tenements rose all about this little air space, all of them filled with ragged, pale-faced children, and red-faced, screaming women, and jabbering foreigners of every nationality. Into the back end of the court a little house had been squeezed, which within its contracted walls accommodated ten or a dozen families. The Lady of Good Cheer turned into the left-hand basement room. Behind the kitchen, which opened on the court, was a dark bedroom. But the chief light in this miserable basement came from a face within it; a face round as the moon at its full, and crimson-tinted as the sunset. Features seemed lost in the ruddy billows of flesh. No scales in the neighbourhood had ever ventured to test the weight of that stout form, but it was assuredly the most remarkable ever seen outside of a museum. The woman greeted the Lady of Good Cheer with a gladness that seemed to irradiate the dull flesh.

"Oh, I'm so glad to see you; I was hopin' you'd come," she said, with a deep sigh of delight. "I'm *so* glad you come."

Her voice had a strange quality, a depth of tone, an intense earnestness and directness that moved strangely those who heard her speak. It was perhaps her absolute simplicity and sincerity that gave her words the charm of those of a little child. Standing beside her the Lady of Good Cheer seemed more slender and fragile than ever, but her firm lips, tightened and compressed by the burden of the day's work, relaxed in a smile, and the deep-set eyes, shadowed by the pain and trouble she had witnessed, brightened with a responsive twinkle.

"Oh, Mrs. Hendrickson, you don't need me any more," she said. "You see I come to you now to get cheered up."

"Sho' now! You're laughin' at me," said Mrs. Hendrickson, with a jolly little giggle that shook her sides. "I was feelin' terrible down-hearted this mornin'."

"Why? Have you had a hard time to-day?" asked the Lady of Good Cheer.

"Oh, you don't know how terrible hard it is for me to be good," she said. "Every time I go out in the yard, the neighbours call me names.

Photo by J. H. Denison.

A RAID IN HAMILTON STREET

They scream out, 'You black Protestant!' 'You old fake,' an' oh, I can't tell you all the vile langwidges they use! It's somethin' fierce. They curse me and call me out o' me name because I won't drink with 'em no more, and it makes me that mad. My! I get crazy! I used to answer 'em back, I could jaw worse than any o' them, but now I put up a prayer in me heart, 'Lord, help me!' I says, and then I feel all quiet an' peaceful like, an' I come back in an' never say a word. They don't know what to think of me, I guess," she shook with a jolly little laugh.

"How is Mr. Hendrickson?" asked the Lady of Good Cheer.

"Oh, he's drinkin' and gamblin', the same's ever. He stops in at the saloon in front and spends more'n half his money on the stuff. But when he comes in, I have the room all neat and clean, and a nice supper for him and I never says nothin' to him. At first he didn't know what to make of it, but now he brings in the beer, and tries to make me drink with him. He knows better, too. He was brought up on the Bible, and he knows a lot more'n I do. If he'd only try, he'd be a heap better'n me."

"He will some day," answered the Lady of Good Cheer. "You know there's nothing aggravates a man so much as to find that his wife is always in the right. He can't make you do wrong now. He can't even make you get angry and call him names. Pretty soon he'll understand that, and then you'll win out."

"Yes, I know," she answered, "but it's so hard to wait. And he's terrible cranky when he's got the drink in him. Sometimes I'm scared o' me life to think of bein' alone with him! But I ain't alone. There's some one with me in me little room, close beside me here, just like you be. It gives me such a peace in me heart — you don't know!"

The round heavy face was illumined now with a light that made the coarse features almost beautiful. It was strange enough and hard to explain, but there was something behind those uncouth, ungrammatical sentences, that took all the absurdity away from her words. No one could listen and not feel that she was describing something that was to her more real than all the hard, cruel facts of the wretched world that surrounded her. No one could look into that face, with its huge cheeks and double chins that seemed made only to wake laughter by its absurdities, without a sense that now she saw something that the rest of the world did not see. There in that miserable basement behind the saloon in the presence of an ignorant uncouth Irishwoman, the unseen world suddenly was made real.

One Sunday some months before, a hideous sodden mass of flesh, reeking with vile alcohol, with bruised face and swollen, swinish eyes, had stumbled into the church and sat down. It was Mrs. Hendrickson. Something in the sermon had touched her. The Lady of Good Cheer found her weeping, and bending over the brutish face, with her delicate hand on the soiled, heavy shoulder, she had spoken a few words of sympathy into ears that none but she would have thought capable of hearing. And something hidden away beneath that coarse mask of flesh did hear and respond.

Nearly every day since, she had called in the wretched basement room, and had seen it change gradually from filth and confusion to neatness and cleanliness. She had given her true self to this ignorant, degraded creature. She had shared with this darkened mind those deep convictions that made her what she was, never doubting but that in some way it would comprehend. It was not so much that she talked about religion and what it could do. There in the dark little basement she talked with Christ, her Master, an unseen Presence, a power to her more efficient than the degenerate heredity and depraved appetites that had mastered this wretched soul, and as she listened, the woman, simple and ignorant as she was, came to feel that Presence in as real a fashion as did the friend who spoke with Him. Her mind was that of a little child, and she received every truth simply and without question.

Mrs. Hendrickson told the Lady of Good Cheer the story of her life. She had been brought up in a wretched hut in Ireland. She laughed at her own ignorance.

"Why, I was that ignorant when I first come over, that I'd never seen a stove, and when they told me to build a fire, sure, I built it on top o' the stove!" and she shook all over with silent laughter.

But there were tragic parts to the story. She had come a simple-hearted child, but she soon began to learn in this new land. She started to drink and curse and carouse. After she married Hendrickson, things went from bad to worse. They were a strangely assorted pair. He was as tall and thin and morose as she was stout and jolly. He was a cooper of Scandinavian descent, who made good wages, but spent all his money on drink and gambling. She surpassed him, however, when it came to drinking. All day long the beer can came and went in her room, until she was nothing but a sodden, brutish mass of flesh. Her first baby she killed by rolling over upon it in a drunken stupor. Her other child grew up to be a fair little girl with blue eyes and flowing, golden hair. She hated the beer can, and would plead with her mother and remonstrate when she saw it brought into the house. One day Mrs. Hendrickson had been drinking heavily. The little girl came in from school, and she sent her down for more beer. The child refused to go, and in drunken fury, her mother seized the little one by her long hair and dragged her head-first downstairs, unmindful of the child's screams of pain. The girl's spine was so injured, that when she died a few months later every one thought it a merciful deliverance. Such a life Mrs. Hendrickson had led,— a life of indescribable bestiality and wretchedness. The change now was so incredible, that as the Lady of Good Cheer looked into her face, and saw the dull, heavy features lit up with a joy and peace that seemed to come from a vision of unseen things, she could hardly believe that this was in truth the same body that had once staggered sodden with alcohol into the church.

One afternoon, some months later, the Lady of Good Cheer was busied in the church yard. Her occupation was not a conventional one, but this was not a conventional church yard. She was engaged in swinging from the "scups" some of the solemn German house-wives and dishevelled and jovial Irish mothers who had attended the meeting which she held every Tuesday afternoon. The church yard had been fitted up as a gymnasium for the children of the neighbourhood, and crowds of ragged and tattered little urchins clamoured daily at the gates for admission to the "Scupping School," as they called it. The Lady of Good Cheer had no idea of seeing the mothers neglected in these plans for the children. She had discovered that their enthusiasm for "scupping" was as great as that of their offspring, and she had insisted that when the swings were put up they should be made strong enough to sustain the weight of the stoutest matron of Cherry Hill. The stoutest matron was undoubtedly Mrs. Hendrickson, and the minister spent some anxious hours calculating her weight and designing a framework of sufficient strength to support the strain. His plan was to put a beam entirely across the narrow yard, setting one end in the wall of the church and the other in the wall of the opposite house, and to hang all the swings and trapezes from this. He sent the sexton down to the lumber yards and secured a beam a foot through and twenty-five feet long, and by the strenuous efforts of some ardent members of the Men's Club, it was at last put into position.

The sexton looked up at it as it spanned the wide yard far aloft, and shook his head dubiously. "It's all right fer the kids," he said, "but it'll never hold that there Mrs. Hendrickson; she'll make it crack fer sure."

The next day the Building Inspector appeared. "What are you doing here?" he asked.

The sexton explained, "We're fixin' up one o' these here gymnasies," he said. "I'm tellin' 'em it's all right fer the kids, but there's some of these ladies can't let the scups alone. We've got one here who weighs about 400 pounds, a reg'lar Barnum prize lady, and I'm thinkin' it'll be a bad day fer the old church when she sets down on that there beam."

A grin spread slowly over the face of the inspector.

"How much weight do you reckon that beam will bear at the point over the middle of the yard?" he asked.

"Oh, we was hopin' it would stand 500 pounds, but come to look at it, I'm afraid the old lady will make it crack if she sets down good and hard."

The inspector pulled out his note book and pencil and figured a moment. "At its middle point that beam will bear a stress of 18,000 pounds, so you've got a little margin even if the lady weighs 500. Good morning," he said and departed, leaving the sexton scratching his head.

So the Lady of Good Cheer had no fear in giving free rein to her mothers with the Scups and she was joining heartily in their fun when some one called her aside. In the waiting-room in the church basement she found Mrs. Hendrickson, bareheaded and panting. When she saw the Lady of Good Cheer she burst into tears, gasping incoherently between her sobs: "It's no use! I can't stand it no longer! I can't! I can't! I can't!"

"What is the matter?" asked the Lady of Good Cheer, putting a hand on her shoulder, and soothing her like a frightened child.

"It's my man. He come in just now with a can o' beer. I had the house all tidied up and a nice supper ready, but he never so much as looked at it. He fills up two glasses from the can and says he: 'Here, take yer glass and drink it down, an' no back talk or there'll be trouble. You've done the pious act long enough. I'm sick o' seein' you settin' there like a Chinese image, pointin' the finger at me fer me sins. Come drink it down!' 'Why, John,' says I, 'don't I keep the house up nice? You wouldn't like to go back an' live like pigs the way we used to?' 'I don't care,' says he, 'pigs or no pigs, I'm boss in this house, an' when I say drink, you've gotter drink.' An' I says, 'John, you ain't got no call to be bossin' me. You know I'll eat and drink anythin' to please yer, even if 'twas mud, only I can't break me promise. 'Tain't right to ax me.' 'Right!' he yells. 'I'll teach you what's right, so you won't forgit it neither!' an' he picks up a stick o' wood an' knocks me down an' beats me with it from head to foot. I'm black and blue all over. An' it don't seem as if I could stand it no longer!"

The Lady of Good Cheer felt herself almost blinded by the strong wave of wrath and pain that swept over her. She felt with this poor woman in every fibre of her soul. The struggle to do right and break from the habits of a life time was certainly hard enough without being beaten and cursed for it. It did not seem as if any one could hold out against such odds, and the Lady of Good Cheer felt like crying out: "There is no use in trying to get on with a man so brutally cruel.

You must leave him, before he drags you down with him."

And then the blinding cloud passed, and she saw clearly again.

"Oh, Mrs. Hendrickson," she said, "it is hard! I know just how hard it is! I feel it all just as if the blows had fallen on my own back. The hardest thing in the world to bear is when those whom you love and are trying to help turn on you and mock you and strike you and torture you. That is what our Lord bore. Every great man and true woman has helped to bear that cross, for that is the only way in which the world can be saved. Now you too are bearing it. You are not alone. They all know how it hurts. He, your Lord and Master, has felt every bit of what you feel to-night. It is hard, but it is worth while. He conquered, and you will conquer, and He is with you in it all."

The tears passed and the broad simple face lit up with a sudden light: "Don't I know it! Why, this afternoon, I felt He was right there with me in the room! It was just like as if you was sittin' there with me on the sofa. An' me troubles didn't bother me no more, an' I was that quiet an' peaceful,— you don't know!"

The Lady of Good Cheer saw her return to her dark basement with some misgiving. She had spoken bravely, but there were limits even to her faith, and some things seemed too hard to be accomplished on earth. And yet in spite of her doubts, her prediction came true.

It was about a year later that John Hendrickson, after keeping sober for over six months, stood up before a large crowd that had gathered to welcome him, and joined the church. He was a determined man, and when he once made up his mind, no one could shake him. The men who offered him drink at his work found this out to their cost. When he made a promise, he kept it. He had his faults, like most mortals, and sometimes Mrs. Hendrickson would shake her head ponderously, and say with a profound sigh: "He's a terrible cranky man, John Hendrickson is." But when she said it she was sitting on a finely upholstered sofa in a nicely furnished three room apartment, full of pretty things, and all John Hendrickson's good weekly wage was safe in a vase on the mantel.

Several years later there was a funeral at the church. The Cooper's Union was present in a body, and many others attended, so that the church was well filled. After the service a few words were spoken of a man who had kept his word and conquered himself, and had built for himself a new and happy life out of the ruins of the past. And every one of that crowd of his friends and fellow workmen bore witness to the fact that from the day he made it, John Hendrickson kept his promise.

XVIII

A RING OF GOLD

SHE was a strange figure of a woman as she stood just outside the door listening to the singing. Her clothes were ragged and dirty, and her grey hair was dishevelled. This in itself was not strange, for she stood in the hall of one of the wretched tenements in Cherry Street, and none of the women who had gathered there at the door were remarkable for the immaculateness of their garments or the perfection of their coiffure. Her face was the strange thing about her. It was a face that might have been taken by some process of legerdemain from behind the desk in some old-fashioned New England Country School house, and attached by magic to a body disguised in rags and dirt here in an environment absurdly incongruous. She wore glasses, and her forehead was puckered with those lines of thought with which the illustrator supplies the old time "school marm." Her mouth had a prim little twist to it, and every wrinkle in the open, homely face suggested an immediate background of apple pie, doughnuts and cider.

The Lady of Good Cheer had been holding a little service for a woman who lay desperately ill in the room within, and the unwonted sound of the singing had drawn the neighbours to the open door. They had listened curiously as she spoke to the suffering woman beside her, and with more pleasure to the voices of the girls from the choir as they sang some of the old hymns.

The Lady of Good Cheer started somewhat hurriedly to leave the room. It was a busy day, and she had many meetings before her. But as she came to the door her eye fell upon the listening woman. The strange face, in the midst of ruddy, snub-nosed Celtic countenances and swarthy, wizened Italian faces at once drew her attention. She saw that the woman took a step forward as if to speak, and then sank back with a self-conscious flush. She noticed, too, that there were tears in her eyes and that her lips were trembling. The Lady of Good Cheer suddenly puzzled, stopped abruptly. Only one who had worked for years in Cherry Street could realise how strange a sight was such a face. If one could judge from the woman's garments, she might have been taken for one of those wretched creatures who spend their days in drunken brawls. Her soiled torn dress and the bruise on her cheek spoke plainly of her association with the commonplace scenes of the neighbourhood, but the face told another story. It was with the sense that she was approaching some unaccountable mystery that the Lady of Good Cheer reached out, took her hand gently, and said: "What is it? Can I do anything for you?"

"I know you're the Lady from the church," said the woman, and the Lady of Good Cheer was glad to note that the voice suited the face and not the garments. She could close her eyes and fancy herself standing in some New England farmhouse.

"I've seen you lots of times," she went on, and hesitated. "Ye wouldn't think o' comin' up to my house some day, and singin' some of them hymns, would ye? My man likes to hear singin' and I might get him to stop in. Ye see, to tell the truth, we ain't neither of us been doin' just right, and I guess it's about time we turned over a new leaf. Why, say, when I heard that old hymn, it made me feel turrible. You wouldn't think it, but I used to be a decent woman. I had a good home up in New England, and it makes me ashamed now to look at a good woman like you. I guess if you knew the half of what I've been doin', ye'd take your hand away mighty quick."

She left the room after receiving the promise of the Lady of Good Cheer to visit her, and one of the other women said, in a low voice, "That Mrs. Bronson's a terror! She and her husband fight somethin' fierce. They nearly tore the house down the other day. It's the drink. They live right over me, and yesterday,— well, say, I thought the roof would fall in on my head fer fair! Of all the poundin' and screamin' and swearin'! They had the can goin' all day, and the two of 'em was too drunk to stand on their pins."

A week later the meeting was held in Mrs. Bronson's house as she requested. It was one of the old three-story tenements, with dark halls and broken dilapidated stairs. The rooms were small, and the ceilings were so low as to endanger the head of a tall man. The plaster was cracked, and the wooden floors were worn and uneven. An excited gabbling in high pitched voices, and a strong odour of garlic and stale macaroni were advance agents to notify the visitor that the tenement was crowded with Italians.

The Lady of Good Cheer climbed the rickety stairs to the garret room in front. The door was thrown open at her knock, and there stood Mrs. Bronson, her ragged dress covered with a clean white apron, her grey hair parted and smoothly brushed. Her spectacles were pushed up on her forehead. There was a smile of welcome on her prim mouth, and each separate wrinkle had a benevolent greeting of its own.

"Well, now," she said, "I'm real glad to see you. Come right in!" and then she added in a whisper, "He's here! I got him to stay!"

Behind her loomed a tall, ungainly longshoreman in a blue-check jumper, his ragged trousers held together by a rough leather belt in which was stuck one of the iron hooks used in unloading freight. He had a rugged, weather-beaten face, a bristling moustache, pale blue eyes and a massive jaw. He had plastered down his sandy hair streaked with grey, evidently by a supreme effort.

"He was scairt to stay, because all his clothes are pawned," she went on in a whisper, "but I told him if it was clothes ye were lookin' for, ye'd be goin' up to Altman's."

Bronson came forward, and held out his great hand somewhat awkwardly, and with a self-conscious smile.

"Come right in!" said Mrs. Bronson, greeting the little company of singers that followed the Lady of Good Cheer. "You won't mind the house, will you?" she went on. "It looks terrible bare, but you see we pawned everything last week." A dull red flush crept over her cheek, and she continued hastily, "We've borrowed some chairs from the neighbours, and I guess it'll do."

The room was bare indeed. There was nothing but a rough wooden table, a broken stove, and the borrowed chairs, but the place was clean for the first time in months, and the rough boards shone with hard scrubbing.

It was a very simple little meeting that was held that day in the bare attic of the tenement crowded with curious Italians. They listened to a few of those words from the ancient prophets that still vibrate with the intense consciousness of the vast Power that waits to lift up the fallen and give strength to the weak, a few of the sweet old hymns, and a request for help made very simply to One who was there in the room. That was all, save that the Lady of Good Cheer spoke very briefly about her deepest beliefs in a conversational way, as if she were talking casually with them all.

When the singers had gone, the Lady of Good Cheer remained behind. Mrs. Bronson had been deeply stirred by the meeting, and wished to tell her all the story of the past. It was a sad tale which she heard as she sat in the bare borrowed chair, her erect slender form leaning forward and her hands clasped about one knee, listening in sympathy to the woman whose homely spectacled face seemed so incongruous with the events she described. The woman had left her New England home with the promise of better work in New York, and had found herself deceived and at last turned adrift without a friend in the great city. She told of the desperate struggle for food, how work was offered by men who helped her, only to betray and then cast her off. She told of the shame that kept her from every appeal to friends at home. She told how she went down that terrible road of wretchedness and sin along which hunger forces many a girl to travel to-day. She drank to dull her conscience and to forget. Every day brought her lower, till she had no home but the streets, no refuge but the vilest of all spots on earth, the backroom of a Bowery saloon. One evening she swung open the screened side door, and crept in to sit down at one of the rough beer-splashed tables. Other women sat about her, women with dirty, plumed hats set rakishly on one side, with tattered, mud-clogged skirts, with features swollen and bloated and eyes bleared and watery. Through the door in front they watched the crowd before the bar, a collection of beings from whom every human trace seemed almost effaced. She could see the beggars of Chatham Square, armless and legless, with hideous faked scars on arm and face. She could see tramps and hoboes, unshaved, unwashed, clothed in dirty rags, with vacuous eyes and hanging jaws and trembling hands. They would creep up to each new comer with a piteous, wheedling appeal, "fer jest one more ball." She could see, too, a few well known yeggs and hold-up men with brutal apish features, thick necks and swollen deformed ears, their pockets bulging with black jacks and sandbags, who were waiting here until the hour when they would waylay some drunken sailor. She could hear their curses and vile stories through the open door. She was starving, as were the other dirty, plumed hags beside her, who with forced gaiety were waving their soiled, clawlike hands at the men outside. Her life depended on the chance that some of those brutes would notice her. Her chances were slim, however, for she preserved a certain trim respectability, and shrank back from the bold hoydens about her. A tall fine looking longshoreman elbowed his way through the hoboes and loafers to the bar, and as he secured "the largest glass of beer for a nickel in New York" and carried it to the back room for safe consumption, his eye caught sight of her. He looked at her fixedly, and studied her from the top of her head to the soles of her feet, so closely that she flushed a little. Then he strode over and sat down beside her. "What are you doing in this dive?" he said: "This ain't no place for the likes of you. You come home with me. That'll be better for you than staying here." It was a new type of knight errantry, unfamiliar to Galahad and his friends, but none the less real and true. From that hour he had been faithful to her, and she to him. They started housekeeping and would have fared well enough but for "the drink." When he brought his money home at the week's end, she sallied forth with the "can," and they kept it going until both were beyond the realm of sanity. Both were high tempered, and under the influence of alcohol they behaved like mad creatures. They scratched and tore and struck, and many a time a blow from his fist left her unconscious. Then they had to begin the next week, sore and wounded, with no food and no money and all their possessions pawned.

It seemed like a strange, incredible dream to the Lady of Good Cheer as she listened. It was a tax upon her imagination to believe that this trim old New England "school marm," who sat beside her in spectacles and a white apron, should have been through scenes such as these. It seemed like a drama in which the actors were a misfit. But it was no play to them. The tears were running down the woman's cheeks as she told the Lady of Good Cheer how tired they were of this wretched life.

The man had listened in awkward silence, seated in one of the wooden chairs which seemed absurdly small to support his huge frame. He sought to hide his ragged trousers by cramping his unwieldy length of leg beneath him in ungainly fashion. His wife turned to him for confirmation.

"Yes, me and her has had enough of this life," he said. "We want to start in and do right. I'm goin' to marry her all reg'lar, and we're goin' to cut out the drink."

There was a settled determination about this rugged man with his massive jaw that carried conviction. The face of the Lady of Good Cheer expressed her delight better than words. She assured them of her sympathy, and added: "Why don't you get married to-morrow? I'll get the minister to come down, and you can start in at once."

"No!" said the man emphatically, "my money's all gone. I haven't any decent clothes, and the furniture's all pawned. When we start, we want to start decent, anyhow."

"But I can help you out," said the Lady of Good Cheer, "and the sooner you set wrong right, the better."

"That may be some folks's way," said the man with bluff decision, "but when I do a thing, I mean to do it right, and I mean to do it myself. No offence to you, mum. When I marry her, I'm agoin' to have a decent home to bring her to, and decent clothes to be married in. If we've waited all these years, we can wait a few days more till I get my money and start right when we do start. I haven't got so much money now as would buy a plate o' beans, let alone a weddin' ring."

"Oh, if it's the ring you want, I can get you a little plated one quite cheap," said the Lady of Good Cheer, fearing to risk postponement of the good resolution.

"No," he answered with a firm snap of his massive jaw. "If my wife is good enough for me to marry, she's good enough to have a ring of real gold. And I won't marry her till I can buy her as good a ring as any woman has got in this city."

The Lady of Good Cheer saw it was useless to push the matter, and she respected the man the more for his decision. He realised the greatness of the adventure upon which he was setting forth. Prayer was to him an untried field, but he was not ashamed to kneel with the Lady of Good Cheer before she left, and ask for help that his efforts might not be in vain. He felt that without aid it was beyond his power and that of the woman at his side to set right a life so wrongly begun, and to overcome the habits of years. He was not a religious man, and had not entered a church in years, but the Lady of Good Cheer had given him a conviction that there was a Power that would aid him in such an endeavour honestly made. "Help me and her to start right, this time," he said. "Help us to cut out the drink. We want to be on the square. We want to do right. Help us, for Christ's sake."

It was not many weeks before the Lady of Good Cheer brought the minister down to Bronson's rooms in the Cherry Street tenement. She would never have known them if she had not had a hand herself in their transformation. Neat new furniture, a bright rug, a gay sofa and a hundred little touches here and there had transformed the bare garret into as attractive a little nest as could be found in the ward.

They stood side by side, these two who had come up out of the depths together. The tall longshoreman, clothed now in garments that he thought worthy of the occasion, took the worn hand of the grey-haired woman whom he wished to honour to the utmost of his ability. She stood there clad in the neat grey dress upon which she had toiled all the week, and there was a flush of pride on her wrinkled cheek as she looked up at the man whose simple, reverent love was raising her up out of degradation and shame, and bestowing upon her the greatest gift that woman can receive. Stumblingly but firmly he repeated the old familiar words, which each man takes upon his lips as he receives the woman who is to preside over his home and to whom he entrusts his life and honour, words repeated often at some gorgeous pageant by youthful lips that understand but little the meaning of that great promise that binds two souls together, but never spoken with deeper understanding or truer meaning than here in the tenement attic by the stumbling lips of the rough longshoreman to the worn grey-haired little woman at his side.

"I, James, take thee Ellen, to be my wedded wife, to have and to hold from this day forward, for better, for worse, for richer, for poorer, in sickness and in health, to love and to cherish till death us do part."

He fumbled a moment in his pocket, and then slipped a ring on the worn finger, and bending with a sort of rough reverence toward the grey little woman at his side he repeated with a special emphasis the words: "With this ring I thee wed," and the solemn adjuration with which the sentence closes. When the prayer was ended, he breathed a long sigh.

"Well, we're started on the square now at last, and we mean business," he said to the Lady of Good Cheer, as she came up to shake his hand. "I reckon that ring'll hold us two together as long as there's anythin' left of us, for it's real gold."

XIX

A PRACTICAL JOKE

THE Lady of Good Cheer was climbing with some difficulty the narrow stair that led to the attic of an ancient dwelling-house in Hamilton Street. Once it had belonged to the aristocracy, and the dark stair up which she was feeling her way had led to the servants' quarters. But now the ancient glory was departed. The whole house was falling to pieces, and reeked with the odour of rats and cats and dirty rags and stale beer. It seemed as if the old walls of this respectable family mansion must shudder with horror over the sights and sounds and odours which were its daily experience. Now each room of this whole top floor accommodated an entire household. At the top of the stairs there was a dark attic hall. The Lady of Good Cheer groped her way to one of the doors and knocked. A husky bass voice from within called, " Come in," and she opened the door and looked in upon a wretched little furnished room. The floor was bare, and there was a bed whose dirty covers lay as they had been thrown in the morning, and a deal table with a few dirty dishes, and a large can of beer, half of which had been spilled and was trickling over the greasy boards.

Out of one of the rickety chairs, there rose a tall cumbrous form, which, except for the soiled black skirt that hung about it, had little in its outline to suggest a woman. The red, hairy arm that she stretched out toward the Lady of Good Cheer was bare, for the sleeves of the dirty white jacket that covered her slouchy masculine shoulders were rolled up, and her blouse was unbuttoned, showing the thick rough neck. The Lady of Good Cheer shrank back instinctively from the coarse face blotched with red and disfigured with a beard of curling brown hairs, but a heavy hand grasped her slender fingers and drew her forward. "Come in! Come in!" It was the same raucous voice she had heard before, even less attractive now that she saw the large mouth from which it emanated with the thick lips parted in an affectionate grin that revealed several broken and missing teeth. The woman clung to the hand of the Lady of Good Cheer, fondling it as she pulled her toward a seat.

"Sit down here, beside me!" she said with a leer in her pale blue eyes, half closed beneath their bushy brows. "I'm so glad to have a lady come in that I can talk to as a friend," she went on, while the Lady of Good Cheer watched with helpless fascination the movement of the thick moustached lips, as they opened and closed and smiled in maudlin good will beneath the swollen, hooked nose.

Then with a sudden movement the Lady of Good Cheer freed herself from the grasp of the large hand, and said hurriedly: "I came to see if you would let me send Jennie to the country next week."

The woman looked over to the dark corner where a pathetic ragged little figure was huddled, playing with some dirty bits of cloth.

"Jennie, come here!" she called in her rough bass voice.

The child rose hastily and came towards her. "Yes'm," she said.

She had a thin body and a pale little face with a large mouth which was trembling now as she looked at her mother with frightened eyes.

"Jennie, you don't want to go to the country, do you?" she asked sternly. "You'd rather stay with your mother, and not go away with all those strangers, wouldn't you?"

"Yes'm," said the frightened child.

"You see," said the woman, "I can't get her to leave me. She loves her mother so, she don't want to be out of my sight. And then, I need her too about the house."

"I wish you would let her go," said the Lady of Good Cheer. "She doesn't look strong, and two weeks in the country would make a new girl of her."

The child watched her with pathetic eagerness, but the mother answered. "No, I don't want to send my child off with all those rough good-for-nothing Irish children. I'm poor, and I've seen hard times, but I belong to one of the best families in Boston. You know the Blanks, don't you, who have that big house on Commonwealth Avenue?"

The Lady of Good Cheer admitted that she knew them well by name.

"Well, Governor Blank is my first cousin. You wouldn't think it to look at this room, but I was brought up with the best people in Boston. I've had a lot of trouble, and my husband is an ignorant man. He has no education, and he can't sympathise with me or understand me at all. That's why I'm so glad to have some one come in that I can talk to about the old days."

But the Lady of Good Cheer had no desire to continue the conversation and rose abruptly.

"I'm sorry, but I must go," she said. "I have twenty calls to make this afternoon."

She tore herself from the grasp of Mrs. Stubbs, and shuddered as she groped her way down the stairs. She was conscious of a strong desire to wash her hands and disinfect her brain cells. At the door she met Mr. Stubbs, whose work was slack just then, and who was returning unusually early. His ragged, ill-fitting garments gave him a dejected look, as he stood with hanging head to let her pass. And yet he was a fine figure of a man, well-built and tall, with regular features, a smooth clear cheek, and a forehead that was high and strong, though surmounted by tousled black hair and a broken hat. There was a pathetic look in his brown eyes, that made him look like a big mastiff who has an unsympathetic master.

"Good morning, Mr. Stubbs," said the Lady of Good Cheer. "I have just been up to ask Mrs. Stubbs to let Jennie go to the country, but she does not think she can spare her. I wish you would let her go. She needs the country air."

Mr. Stubbs made no response, but shook his head dubiously.

"Won't you persuade Mrs. Stubbs to let her go?" she asked.

"I'd like her to go first rate," he said, "but if she says no, there's an end on't," and he went on up stairs with a weary drag to his ill-shod feet, leaving behind him an odour of stale beer and ancient rags. He was a teamster and made good wages, but whatever financial securities he acquired were at once liquidated by Mrs. Stubbs, who kept him saturated with "the drink." Little Jennie was essential in the scheme of things as a means of transport between the corner saloon and the attic room, and her small legs were kept in constant motion over the familiar route. She could not be spared to go to the country. She was allowed no outings or amusements.

Once, some months later, the Lady of Good Cheer met Jennie playing with a rough crowd of children in Cherry Street, but even then the inevitable can was in her hand, and she was evidently stealing a few moments of play en route. The children were playing in front of a house where a little girl had just died, and over their heads as they shouted and laughed hung the pathetic white rosette, soiled and tattered, that told of one more little life crushed out by the insidious, destroying forces of the great city.

It may have been in part the effect of that symbol, but it seemed to the Lady of Good Cheer that little Jennie had suffered a horrifying change. The small face that had been so thin and pathetic seemed swollen and red with many blotches. Her large mouth had grown coarse and her lips thick. Her manner was no longer shy, but bold and rough. The Lady of Good Cheer feared that here were the signs of a death far more terrible than that symbolised by the white bow beneath which the child was playing, and determined to make another effort to get her out of the clutches of Mrs. Stubbs. Mr. Stubbs had joined the Men's Club. The Lady of Good Cheer had persuaded him to take the pledge, and for some time he kept sober. His chronic environing atmosphere of stale alcohol seemed to have been dissipated. Mrs. Stubbs had also renounced her beer with many solemn protestations and the Lady of Good Cheer in return had enabled them to move from furnished rooms into an apartment of their own.

But the Lady of Good Cheer had little confidence in the virtuous protestations of Mrs. Stubbs, and she was convinced that she was using all her influence in an underhand way to drag down her husband and child. She always felt an instinctive dread of an encounter with Mrs. Stubbs, and it was not until her conscience urged it that she realised that a call could no longer be postponed. Accordingly one day she entered the narrow court, and ascended the stairs of the rear house in which Mrs. Stubbs' new apartment was located. As she entered the little room, she was at once aware of an atmosphere unduly alcoholic, and the overwhelmingly affectionate greeting of Mrs. Stubbs strengthened the impression that Mrs. Stubbs was up to some villainy. The woman clung to her hand with a maudlin grin, and the Lady of Good Cheer had an irresistible desire to screen herself from the leer of her pale blue eyes, beneath their bushy brows, as from something unclean and polluting.

Mrs. Stubbs was in an affectionate and confidential mood. She spoke of her proud family connections, and of the troubles and injustice of human life.

"I oughtn't to be living like this," she said. "I'm an educated woman, and a woman of good family. I'd never have ought to take up with a man like Mr. Stubbs." She paused a moment and then leaned forward with a wink of her pale blue

Photo by J. H. Denison.

THE SIGN OF DEATH

eyes. " I'll tell you something. You think I'm married to Mr. Stubbs, but I ain't. I wouldn't marry an ignorant good-for-nothing man like that. I can leave him any time I want to."

The Lady of Good Cheer felt a wave of disgust run through her, but she mastered it.

" I'm very sorry to hear that," she said. " If you aren't married to him, you ought to leave him at once."

" Oh, no! " she answered, with another wink. " Not just now. He brings in too good pay. But some day, I will. I'm not a-going to spend my whole life with a man like that."

The Lady of Good Cheer left with an overmastering sense of disgust and horror, and it was not diminished when she met Mr. Stubbs walking with erratic steps and with a vacant expression in his brown eyes.

" Come in to the church house a minute," she said, " I want to speak with you."

Mr. Stubbs shambled into the waiting room and dropped loosely into a seat.

" I'm afraid things are not going very well at your house," she began.

Ordinarily it was like drawing crocodile's teeth to extract a word from Mr. Stubbs, but to-day under alcoholic pressure, the safety valve was opened and all the imprisoned bitterness of months came pouring forth.

" It's something fierce! " he said. " I don't

know what to do with that woman. She drives me crazy."

The Lady of Good Cheer felt much sympathy with the man. His silent, uncomplaining loyalty to the woman he had chosen, and his hard toil on her behalf, indicated something of nobility in the man. She felt that Mrs. Stubbs was deceiving him and exploiting his hard labour, and that her degrading influence was dragging him down to lower and lower depths. There was no hope for him while this woman kept him in her clutches. If he were free from her, he might prosper and the fine qualities in him so long suppressed, might enable him to develop into a really useful man.

"She told me you were not married to her. Why don't you leave her and start in for yourself?"

Mr. Stubbs looked at her with a slow surprise in his sad brown eyes.

"Leave her?" he repeated. For a moment his face lit up. Then he shook his head. "No," he said, "there's the little girl. We've got to stick together for the little girl's sake. She's all I've got, and I couldn't have no harm come to her."

The Lady of Good Cheer offered to provide for the child. She brought every possible argument to bear, but he only shook his head slowly.

"No," he said, "I've lived with her these ten or twelve years, an' I ain't a goin' to run off and leave her. It would make trouble for the little girl."

"For the little girl's sake then, you must keep straight and stop drinking. If you don't, there will be no one to look out for her."

"I know," he said, "but, my God! what can I do? You don't know that woman! It don't seem as if I could keep from the drink when she's around!"

The Lady of Good Cheer did her best to make him feel her sympathy and respect. Indeed, in this ignorant workingman, she seemed to recognise a higher sense of honour, and a more heroic standard than that of the world's chivalry. Because a woman had once surrendered herself to him, he felt himself bound to give her his whole life and all that he could earn, even though she had become hideous to him and he knew that she abused his devotion and despised him for his loyalty.

The Lady of Good Cheer was so anxious about little Jennie that she made another effort to see Mrs. Stubbs. She found that lady even more affectionate and confiding than on her previous visit. She made an earnest plea that the child should be allowed to go away to the country, and Mrs. Stubbs seemed inclined to relent.

"I'll tell you a secret about that child, only you must promise never to tell," she said with a leer. "Mr. Stubbs thinks the world o' that child, and he sticks by the home just for her sake. He thinks she's his child "— and she leaned forward till the coarse lips and hairy chin were close to her listener and winked with her pale blue eyes —" but she ain't! " she concluded with a hoarse laugh. " That's one on him! I've fooled him all these years! Ain't that a great joke? "

XX

A BATTLE WITH DEMONS

"WHY don't you go in next door and help them two little girls?" said Mrs. O'Brien to the Lady of Good Cheer one day when she was calling in the tallest and narrowest and dirtiest of the tenements in the "Long Block." "Their mother's dead, an' their father's a howly terror! Sure, I'm that flustrated wid his rowin' and jawin' next door that I've got palpytashuns in me chist an' cole shivers in me backbone. He near kilt the two of 'em this afternoon. I heard an awful screech, and run in thinkin' the kid had threw a fit or somethin', an' up jumps that man wid a knife as long as an umbrell! An' says he, 'What are ye doin', buttin' in here! Git out o' me house, an' quick too,' says he, 'or ye'll be ridin' over to Brooklyn in a hearse wid yer skin so full o' holes your own grandmither won't know yer.' I let out a yell: 'Howly Mither! Save us!' says I, and run for me life. I'd no more leave that man to take care o' two girls, than I'd leave a wild Indian to nurse me baby wid a scalpin' knife. It ain't respectable!"

The Lady of Good Cheer knocked at the next door and it was opened by a slim, wiry girl of seventeen. Her freckled face showed evidence of close contact with the world's coarse thumb in the hard lines about her mouth, and in the suspicion and defiance that filled her eyes, as though some bitter experience of human nature were written forever in them.

"What do you want?" she demanded, abruptly.

The Lady of Good Cheer explained her position, and told the girl she knew of their trouble and would be glad to help if she could.

Her defiant manner gave way at once. "Come in," she said. "Oh, I don't know what to do! Me father's clean out of his head! I don't care for myself, but he shan't hurt Nellie," and a tigerish glint came into her eyes that told the Lady of Good Cheer that the child would not suffer so long as her sister had nails and teeth.

The rooms were clean and in good order, and furnished with many of those little knick-knacks that are the record of a family life, and often link a wretched present with happy associations of the past. By the window stood a little girl of about eight years with a face of such unusual loveliness that the Lady of Good Cheer looked at her in surprise. Her features were regular, save for a slight saucy tilt to the nose. She had the large liquid blue eyes, and those red full lips chiseled in the form of Cupid's bow, which are seldom found, save in the imagination of a pre-Raphaelite. A mass of dark hair, with a glint of gold in it when it caught the light, fell over her shoulders and curled round her delicate cheek. Just now the corners of her mouth drooped pathetically and there were tears in her eyes.

"Tell me all about it," said the Lady of Good Cheer.

The girl's eyes filled with angry tears as she described a battle fought between maddened brute strength and clinging childish devotion for the possession of a mother's watch, the sole memorial and keepsake left to these motherless girls to recall a vanished love and care. The father had seized all the money Jessie had saved to pay the rent, and had come home more crazed with drink than before to demand this one article which the girls prized above all else. Indignantly Jessie had refused to give it up to be pawned, and the infuriated man had rushed at her with curses, and struck her. She was not to be cowed by words or even by blows, and she had defended her sacred relic desperately, until in an outburst of rage the madman threw her to the ground, and, catching up a carving knife from the table, thrust it at her throat. Then she yielded, but it was with tears of anger rather than fear. It would not take him long to spend the money he received from the pawnbroker. She was expecting him to return at any moment to demand some of Nellie's trinkets or some of the household belongings.

"An' I've worked so hard to keep the house together," said the girl with the hot tears still in her eyes. "An' if he goes on like this, there won't be a thing left in a day or two! An' me and Nellie haven't had a thing to eat all day!" she added.

"It's my birthday, too!" chimed in Nellie. Her long-lashed eyes filled again with tears, and her delicate red lips quivered. "I'm eight to-day and I thought he'd bring me such a nice present! He said he'd give me a fine time on my birthday, an' I've been crying all day."

The story was sad enough, indeed, but the Lady of Good Cheer saw in it an even tragic significance. The situation was acutely dangerous. Aside from the risk that the man in his crazed condition might seriously injure one of these defenceless children, there was the probability that he would carry out the threat he had made to Jessie to bring home with him some of his drunken companions and carouse with them all night, leaving the two girls at the mercy of a roomful of intoxicated men. The Lady of Good Cheer briefly considered the matter, then she went out swiftly, promising to return in a moment. First she sent a message to the church for reinforcements. Then she bought some food, which included a birthday cake for Nellie.

Nellie's eyes glowed at sight of the cake and when the candles were lighted, her joy knew no bounds. They were in the midst of a jolly little birthday party, when they heard a heavy stumbling step on the stair. "He's coming!" cried the girls. For the Lady of Good Cheer the situation was a dangerous one. No one had come to her aid. To face alone a man who was so mad with drink that he had tried to kill his own children is hardly a pleasant task, and this man was a desperate character, who in his present mood would not hesitate a moment to strike a woman or knock her down. Yet retreat never entered her mind. If her heart beat more rapidly as she waited to see what sort of a creature it was with which she had to deal, no one could have detected it.

In a moment the door was thrown violently open, and a huge man entered with the lurching, swinging stride of a sailor. He had been fighting, his coat was torn, a heavy blow on the cheek bone had caused a swelling that made his eyes seem narrower and more piglike than ever, and his drooping, sandy moustache had a stain of blood upon it. He was from the North of Ireland, and his origin was evident in his speech, thickened though it was by drink.

"Gi' me s' money, Jessie," he shouted, "gotter have s' money!"

"I haven't got none," said Jessie sullenly.

"Yes, ye have, too! don't give me no back talk! I know yer tricks!" and he advanced upon her with doubled fist.

The Lady of Good Cheer rose and stepped forward with a swift movement that brought her between the enraged man and his daughter.

"Good evening, Mr. Sanderson," she said.

He had been so absorbed in his quest for the money that he had paid no attention to her. Now he turned upon her with surprise and wrath. The veins on his forehead thickened. With that sullen scowl on his face he was as ugly a beast as ever assumed a human shape, and many a strong man would have thought twice before pursuing the conversation.

"What're ye doin' here?" he shouted. "Teachin' my girls to disobey their father. I'll teach you to butt in."

He gave a quick lurch toward her. His movements had the uncertain and violent suddenness of a man maddened by alcohol. In another moment he would have struck her down, as he had just knocked down two men who barred his way in the saloon. She faced him, tall and slender, with head erect. Her aquiline nostrils quivered a little, and her firm lips tightened slightly, but from beneath her high brow her deep, steady eyes, unflinching and calm, looked him full in the face.

"Mr. Sanderson," she said quietly, "I know you are a gentleman, and that you would never do anything discourteous to a lady."

With those eyes upon him, the drunken brute faltered. His hands sunk to his side. A foolish smile, half of embarrassment, half of conceit, came over his face. "A gentleman? Yes, sure I'm a gentleman!" he said. He gave his shoulders a sudden hunch, as if his coat were too tight for them, and expanded his chest in imitation of the person of quality he was supposed to resemble. Then he let out a cracked and maudlin laugh, that sounded like the crow of a hoarse rooster.

The girls looked on, amazed that he had not struck down their visitor. He could hardly account for it himself. When he rushed at any one with his huge fist poised, he was accustomed to see either fear or rage in his victim's eyes, and then it was easy to strike. But in these eyes there was no trace of fear nor rage, nor yet that more maddening expression of disgust and contempt. They were challenging him on a point of honour, as if they refused to accept him at his face value. They seemed to question and probe, but not to laugh at him. There was almost a reverence in them. He felt she had found in him something that deserved respect, and it pleased him. He paid little attention to her words, but the sympathy in her voice arrested him. She was not fault-finding, as other women were. Vague images out of the past rose before his bleared eyes: the image of a white-haired woman by the fireside, whose hands were stretched out to bless him, the vision of a fair-faced bride who long ago had trusted him and believed him true. The Lady of Good Cheer talked on of his home, and of little Nellie, and of her disappointment that her birthday had been forgotten.

"Poor little Nellie!" said Sanderson, maudlin tears coming into his eyes. "Shure, 'tis a shame! It's a bad day she's had for sure! Never mind, dearie, your dad'll give you a fine present some day! But I'm too poor now. I'm out o' work. What can a man do? Dear! dear! it's terrible!" and he gave a long sigh.

"You see we have a birthday cake, anyway," said the Lady of Good Cheer. "Isn't that nice? Sit down and join the party."

"No," said Sanderson, "I must go."

A sudden fierceness came into his face, and he turned to Jessie. "Now give me that money! I've got to have it! I won't stand no foolin'!"

He lifted his huge fist again. For the moment he was out of the range of the glance by which the Lady of Good Cheer had held him.

"Mr. Sanderson!" she called.

Her voice, though quiet, was so firm and authoritative that Sanderson turned, expecting a tirade and preparing to face it with a burst of rage. But instead of a scolding he met a glance of grateful confidence that seemed to thank him for his quick understanding and prompt response. She seemed so sure that no further word could possibly be necessary, that he gave a gasp of astonishment. Before he could speak she was inquiring in a tone of great sympathy how he had come to lose his position as pressman, and to meet with such hard luck. There is nothing a drunken man loves more than to dilate on his misfortunes, and Sanderson, willing to be beguiled, sank down on the sofa.

"Hard luck! Yes! Ah me! Ochone! Yes! I've had nothin' but hard luck. I believe the divil is afther me!" His eyes, half bleared with drink, seemed to catch a strange glint of terror.

"Did ye ever see the divil, now?" he asked in a thick whisper. "I did; or somethin' like him."

"Tell me about it," said the Lady of Good Cheer, thankful to have led his mind away from drink, even though it was to the devil.

"It was a few months ago. We was livin' in Catherine Street in some rooms we got cheap because a dago got murdered there, and they said the rooms was haunted. An' one night we'd been having a bit of a jolly time, an' I went into me room and laid down on me bed. Pretty soon the lights began to go out, an' I thinks, 'That's funny!' but I stays on me bed. An' it gets darker an' darker, an' by an' by I sees the door openin' slow an' still like." His voice sunk to a thick whisper.

"An' through the door come a man, the biggest man I ever see, big an' black, he was. An' he comes nearer an' nearer, an' shure he had no head at all, at all! An' I tried to yell, an' I couldn't open me head, an' I tried to jump up an' I couldn't move so much as me finger. An' the cole sweat was pourin' off me in streams! On he come, an' I sees he had his head in his hands,— all drippin' blood, it was. An' he comes right up to me,— shakin' like a leaf I was,— an puts the head right down on me chist! An' wid that I gives out a yell like a fire engine, an' jumps off the bed and runs clean through the house an' out into the street! An' when we went back the man was gone. I moved out o' the house pretty quick, but the bad luck follers me. Ah me! Ochone! the divil is after me! Shure that's the trouble!"

"Is it?" she asked, with a smile. "I'm afraid the trouble is that you don't really want to get away."

He sprawled with his huge length over the sofa, and she began to speak seriously and sympathetically of the life he had been living. She told him plainly what she thought of his behaviour, and he sat quietly and listened, although he would have knocked a man down for saying half as much. For he felt that, though she rebuked him, it was because she had found something in him she respected and trusted, and he recognised that she had a right to speak as she did. It was the same right which he had acknowledged in those who years ago had believed in him — the claim which faith and love always have over a man's life. The battle was won long before help came, and the girls were safe that night from terrors worse than death. On her way uptown the Lady of Good Cheer ended her account of the evening by saying: "I don't care what you say! I like Mr. Sanderson. There's something that's really worth while at the bottom of that man."

XXI

A STRANGE DISCIPLINARIAN

"SAY, won't ye come over to my house and see me mommer?" said little Annie, slipping her hand into that of the Lady of Good Cheer, as they came out of the mission in Rutgers Street together. Annie was a mystery which the Lady of Good Cheer had never solved. She had a bright, elfish face, and shining, dark eyes, and a tangle of brown hair. She was eight years old, but very small and delicate in every outline. Her dress was in rags, she was barefoot, and her thin face was white and pinched, but she was not in the least the ordinary street urchin. She had a quick intelligence and an affectionate disposition which made her a favourite with her teachers in school, but she had also a strange atmosphere of another and totally different life, much as the odour of violets might cling to a broken bottle in an ash heap. She seemed to the Lady of Good Cheer like an elfin changeling, a quaint little fairy princess that some old witch had dropped into the most wretched poverty-stricken block in the swarming tenement district.

The Lady of Good Cheer had never been able to learn where she lived, or anything about her parents, and she was therefore surprised and delighted at this informal invitation. Annie had dropped in at a children's meeting held in a mission which had recently been started in the block, and she and the Lady of Good Cheer had soon become good friends. When general topics of conversation were introduced, she was a great chatterbox, but if any question led up to the subject of her parents or her home, she would become suddenly silent, and stand with shyly drooping head until the danger was past. To-day, however, for some reason she had broken the taboo. Her elder sister looked down at her with astonishment and rebuke in her face and apparently started to check her, but shyness was too strong in her, and she only flushed deeply and shifted from one bare foot to another as she patted the baby in her arms, who had opened his mouth in preparation for a good howl. He was an enormous baby with a grimy red face protruding from the wrappings of a dirty grey shawl, and it took all Gertrude's slight strength with the assistance of occasional desperate hitches to keep the huge animated bundle from wriggling to the ground. Gertrude was a beautiful child, as much advanced in her physical development as Annie was backward. Though but twelve years old her form already showed the rounded outlines of a perfect maidenhood. She had deep violet eyes and long lashes, and she surveyed the Lady of Good Cheer dubiously. A soft flush played on her rounded cheek, delicate as a rose leaf, and her red lips were parted in a doubtful smile that showed her pretty white teeth. As the Lady of Good Cheer looked at her and noticed the ragged, dirty dress and soiled hands, the streak of smut across the piquant little nose, she felt more than ever the strange mystery that surrounded these children, so evidently of good parentage and quick intelligence, and kept them in such conditions of poverty and filth.

Annie clung to her hand and danced gaily at her side, and Gertrude followed with reluctant steps, carrying her heavy burden, and the Lady of Good Cheer crossed the street and entered an ancient dilapidated tenement that seemed on the verge of dissolution. Up the broken wooden steps they went, and Annie burst open a door in the rear, and flew in like a whirlwind.

"Mommer!" she cried. "Here's the lady from the mission come to see you!" The woman who rose from an uncertain rocking chair to meet her was one who would have drawn the attention of the Lady of Good Cheer anywhere. She was well formed, and there was a certain dignity about her person. Her cheeks were fair and smooth, and her regular features and her rosy complexion gave her a surprisingly youthful air. Her pale yellow hair had been fastened in a knot, but most of it had escaped and hung about her forehead and neck in stray locks. Her ragged dress was open at the throat, and was so soiled that its original hue would have been hard to determine. Her feet were bare, for it was a hot summer's day.

"I'm glad to see you," she said. "Come right in and sit down."

Her red lips, parting in a smile of welcome, disclosed a missing tooth or two. But none of these superficial deficiencies seemed to embarrass her in the least. She might have been a hostess in full dress welcoming her guests to a Fifth Avenue mansion.

The room was in hopeless confusion. Although the greasy debris of the last meal had not been cleaned away, the table was half set for a new meal with plates and knives and forks which had apparently had no close contact with the dishpan since the last occasion of their usefulness. An old dirty comforter lay in one corner, and each chair was occupied by ragged garments or by voluminous wrappings, apparently discarded by the baby when hopelessly soiled and awaiting some laundry day in the uncertain future. In the midst sat a large pan of beans prepared for the evening repast.

The Lady of Good Cheer made the necessary remarks in the way of salutation, but the more she looked about, the more she was impressed by the amazing incongruity of the scene. How had this woman and these children, so evidently belonging to a different sphere in life, sunk to this level of wretchedness and degradation? Certainly there was a mystery here. What could the father and husband of this family be like? A hopeless drunkard he surely must be, to have dragged them down to this.

"Annie's told me a lot about you," said Mrs. Dexter, "and I'm right glad to see you. She thinks there's nobody in the world like you. Now you're here, won't you sit down and take a bite to eat with us? Mr. Dexter will be coming in soon, and I'd like to have you see him."

The Lady of Good Cheer was anxious to see Mr. Dexter, but the greasy table and the unduly familiar relations between the bean-pot and the garments of the sick baby dissuaded her.

"I am afraid they are expecting me at home," she said. "I must be going."

"We aren't rich, and can't give you a fine dinner, but you aren't too proud to sit down with poor folks like us, are you?" said Mrs. Dexter, flushing a little and looking at her suspiciously.

The Lady of Good Cheer was exceedingly anxious to win her confidence and saw she had made a false step.

"Indeed I'm not," she said, "and I should like above all things to meet Mr. Dexter. If it's not too much trouble, I'll stay and I can send word to the church that I'll be delayed."

"That's fine now," said Mrs. Dexter, a pleased smile at once banishing the suspicion and wounded pride from her face. "Here comes Hughey, and

Mr. Dexter will be in in a minute. If you get a chance, see if you can't get Mr. Dexter to go to work. He's an A-one engineer, and can make big money, but he had a row with the Union, and now I can't get him even to try for a job. If it wasn't for Hughey, who's driving for Hecker's mills over there, we'd all starve. It isn't much he brings in, but it's enough to keep us in beans."

Was this the explanation — a row with the Union? The Lady of Good Cheer became more anxious than ever to see Mr. Dexter. Just then there was a step in the hall and the door opened.

"Here he is!" said Mrs. Dexter, and then to her husband, "This is the lady from the mission that Katy is always talking about, and she's going to stay to supper."

Mr. Dexter was a tall man with a good figure. He was dressed in a black suit which was threadbare but scrupulously neat, and his collar was white. His dark hair was streaked with grey. As the Lady of Good Cheer noticed his high forehead, his brown eyes set deep under heavy brows, his straight nose and full firm chin, and she set aside at once the hypothesis of the hopeless drunkard. His mouth was covered by a heavy black moustache, but his features showed not only intelligence, but self-command and firm determination. He looked at the Lady of Good Cheer, and then gave a rapid glance about the room. A frown darkened his face, as his eyes finally rested on the dishevelled costume of his wife. In one swift look he surveyed her from her tangled yellow locks to her bare soiled feet.

"I should think you could have fixed things up a bit before asking a lady to supper," he said sternly.

"Oh, she isn't proud," said Mrs. Dexter. "She isn't ashamed to sit down with poor folks. He's always like that," she went on to the Lady of Good Cheer. "He's always finding fault with the house in some way. But so long as he isn't working, I don't see what I can do about it."

He looked at her a moment with stern, cold eyes, and seemed about to speak; then he turned to the Lady of Good Cheer.

"Well, I'm glad you've come, anyway," he said, "and I'm sorry we have nothing better to offer you."

They sat down and Mrs. Dexter heaped the soiled plate in front of the Lady of Good Cheer with an enormous portion of the suspected beans. It was a trying ordeal. The Lady of Good Cheer toyed with her food, and conversed vigorously. Then, availing herself of a moment when Mrs. Dexter had returned to the stove and Mrs. Dexter had gone to the other room to get some papers to show her, she slid the beans dexterously from her plate into a pail of refuse that stood at hand. Mrs. Dexter seemed a little astonished and much pleased at her rapid consumption of her meal, and begged to be allowed to fill her plate again, but she declined with grace and firmness. In the conversation Mr. Dexter showed much intelligence. He was an engineer of the first grade and showed her the certificates of his capacity in hydraulics, pneumatics and electricity, as well as in the lower grades. She tried to discover the reason for his being out of work, and he told a long story of some unjust demand of the Union for the payment of a tax which he had refused. They had then "done him out of his job," and he had refused to pay his dues, with the result that he was now ruled out from all Union jobs in the city.

The determined character of the man showed in the story. If he thought he was wronged, he would undoubtedly go to any length rather than give in, but the Lady of Good Cheer was more and more convinced that this was not the root of the difficulty. When she offered to interview certain persons who would set him right with the Union, he met her proposition evasively. She changed the subject, and spoke of the children. He said that though he was a Catholic he did not mind having the children go to the mission. His wife was a Protestant and he thought they would get no harm from going to a meeting now and then. This opened up a new possibility. In the experience of the Lady of Good Cheer, the most degraded families were those in which there was a mixed marriage. Things usually went well enough with the married pair until the children were born, then there was a violent dispute as to their baptism and as to what church they should attend, which after years of bitterness usually resulted in the compromise that they should go to no church and have no religion, and after this the degeneration of the family life seemed to be invariable.

Some disagreement of this sort might easily have occurred with such a determined man as Dexter. But the more she talked with him, the more she was convinced that he was too broad-minded to wreck his life through religious bigotry. He had a simple, reverent belief in God, but he showed much contempt for the conventional practices of religion. He even said he should like to have the children attend Sunday School. The Lady of Good Cheer turned away from the house more perplexed than ever, deeply convinced that it was some strange mystery which kept this man of first class ability living in filth in a wretched tumble-down tenement among the worst hoodlums and brawlers of the ward.

The Lady of Good Cheer set herself to win Dexter's confidence, but he was a sensitive and very reserved man, and she found it almost impossible to penetrate the barrier which he seemed to have raised about his thoughts and purposes. She knew, from the way in which he had looked about the room, that the filth of his home was as repulsive to him as to her; and from his expression as his eyes rested on his wife, she knew that it was not his wish that a woman with her natural attractions should go about looking like a scarecrow or a beggar. And this knowledge rendered the situation more and more inexplicable.

It was some months later that the Lady of Good Cheer knocked at the door of the Dexters, and heard from within Mr. Dexter's voice raised in angry expostulation. She entered to find him standing indignantly over Mrs. Dexter, who was seated at the table and had succeeded in half screening a large pail of beer behind a newspaper. There was a moment's silence, and then Dexter broke out.

"Well," he said, "you've come at a good time. Don't try to hide the can," he said to his wife. "She might just as well know right now what you're up to.

"What do you think?" he went on to the Lady of Good Cheer. "That woman had a nice little house of her own and a pretty garden and everything she wanted. Her children were well dressed, and there wasn't a thing she asked for that she didn't get. But whenever my back was turned, in came the can. And when I came back from work, the house was dirty, the table littered up with grease and dirt, the children all covered with dirt, and she herself looked like a scarecrow. I talked to her, and lectured her. I got angry and scolded, and not a bit of good did it do. I tried everything I knew, and things only got worse, and at last I said: 'If you want to live like a pig, like a pig you shall live,' and I threw up my job and sold out my house and moved over here to the worst tenement in Rutgers Street, and here we've been ever since. She didn't think I meant business, but at last when the money was all gone, one day after she'd seen you, she promised to cut out the can, and I was going to work again; but here I come in and find her old friend sitting on the table as usual. It's no use. What can you do with a creature like that?" he cried, pointing at the ragged dishevelled woman whose fair cheeks had flushed a deep crimson, as she bit her red lips and twisted a straggling lock of her yellow hair.

Dexter was evidently beside himself with indignation and despair, for in all these months, the high-strung, sensitive man had never spoken a word in disparagement of his wife.

This, then, was the mystery! Why had she not suspected it before? And yet it was not an ordinary occurrence for a man who had all the things which the world seeks, to renounce them all and to sit down in rags with his family, in order to teach them a moral lesson. No wonder the mystery was difficult to penetrate.

It was long before the Lady of Good Cheer left them that day, but before she retired she had won one of her great victories, and she held the articles of capitulation in her hands. A contest with a man of such intelligence and firmness was no light matter. The Lady of Good Cheer sat with her slender form poised on the edge of a chair, leaning forward and clasping her hands about one knee. Her hat was pushed back impatiently a little from her high brow, and her deep-set eyes, full of comprehending sympathy, were fixed upon Dexter's face, while she put up a plea with all the earnestness that was in her, that this stern, disappointed man should still have a little faith in his wife and make another trial. When she went away she had made a compact. She had agreed to make Mr. Dexter a loan which would establish him with the Union, and he agreed to go back to work upon the condition that the Lady of Good Cheer should guarantee that his wife would turn over a new leaf and cease from drinking, and keep up the house in as decent a condition as could be reasonably expected.

Dexter kept his part of the contract. It was a desperately hard struggle. He had offended some of the dignitaries in the Union, and they rejoiced to humble him by keeping him in line many months waiting for a job, and then passing him over when the better opportunities arrived. But he pocketed his pride, bitter though it was to him, and at last he secured a job as engineer in a large brewery. He moved into better quarters, and thanks to the frequent visits of the Lady of Good Cheer, there was a marked change in his home. But he had many back debts to pay, and he would not spend a penny in fitting up his own home until these were all settled.

The Lady of Good Cheer visited the family at frequent intervals, inspected the condition of the house, and applied a little tactful stimulus to Mrs. Dexter, whenever she discovered danger of a relapse. Mrs. Dexter did her utmost to stand well with the Lady of Good Cheer. One day, when the Lady of Good Cheer knew the Dexters had been having an especially hard time with far too little food, Annie appeared at the church with a large tin can. She came up slowly to the Lady of Good Cheer, a tiny figure wrapped in an old shawl, which concealed the deficiencies in her dress. Her head drooped, and she looked up sideways out of the corner of her eyes.

"Me Mommer sent you this," she said. "Me cousin from Long Island brought them over to us, and me Mommer said I was to take them all up to you."

The Lady of Good Cheer opened the pail and saw that it was filled with fine, fat frog's legs. She was deeply touched by this self-sacrificing act on the part of the Dexters, this wish to hand over to her a bit of choice food when they were on the edge of starvation. She answered with feeling.

"Thank you, ever so much, Annie. I don't know when I've had a gift that I appreciated more, but I can't take them all. I'll take out some and send the rest back for you to eat."

"Oh, never mind!" said Annie, looking up in some alarm, "me Mommer said they might pizen us!"

Month after month passed, and lengthened into years. Gertrude had grown into a charming maiden of fifteen, full of life and of the love of pleasure, natural to her age and sex. But the old régime continued. She still wore an old threadbare gown, and it was still her lot to tend the baby, a new one now, all day. Her mother even at her best was never an active housewife, and most of the hard cleaning and washing and scrubbing fell upon Gertrude. If she had been permitted to go out for a little fun after her work was finished, she would probably have remained satisfied to slave; but after cruel drudgery to be turned out in the street in a soiled old dress with a huge howling burden to carry about wherever she went was a trying lot for a girl who was gradually beginning to realise that she was beautiful enough to command the attention of every man in the block. There are limits beyond which the flexible nature of a girl, beautiful, high-tempered, and full of the passion of life, cannot be bent; and so it came about that after the baby was put to bed in the evening, Gertrude often slipped away, and it was sometimes late before she returned. Her father was on night work at the time. Mrs. Dexter never dared to tell her husband of Gertrude's escapades, and the girl was a silent child who never spoke of what concerned her alone. Her mother could not extract a syllable as to where she had been. Dexter was working night and day in the effort to pay off his debts, and the hard labour left its traces upon his health. During those days of hunger and destitution in the filth of Rutgers Street, the White Death, the terrible scourge of the tenements, had laid its hand upon him. Every day he came back paler and thinner, a dry cough shook him, and his temper became more and more uncertain.

One night Dexter returned unexpectedly from work at ten o'clock. Gertrude was out, and he gradually drew from the frightened mother the story of the past months. He had come back from work exhausted, but as he grasped the truth, a tide of furious indignation swept through him. His hollow eyes flashed unpleasantly, and a spot of colour showed on his haggard cheek. He tramped restlessly up and down the bare wooden floor of the kitchen, biting his moustache and awaiting the girl's return, while his wife sat by tearful and dishevelled, trying, to disarm his wrath by occasional ejaculations. It was nearly midnight, when they heard a light foot-fall on the stair, the door was thrown open and Gertrude stood before them, looking very pretty in the long, red cloak that was flung over her shoulders. Her delicate cheeks were glowing, and her long-lashed eyes flashed with excitement. She stopped in sudden terror as she saw her father. She turned white and shrank back in dismay.

"Where have you been?" said her father in low, stern tones.

His face was ghastly white now, and his eyes flamed with a dangerous light. She stood in silence, and slowly the little head she had held so haughtily with the piquant nose in air, sunk down upon her breast.

"Come, girl, tell me where you've been!"

The low tones of his voice cut like a whip and still she made no answer. He sprang forward, and seized her by the wrist, and with a sudden jerk dragged her cloak from her. Then he stepped back in wrath and disgust. She wore the garments used by the girls who dance in the low Bowery dives. Sudden uncontrollable anger flamed in his brain. While he was seeking to restore his home and his name to honour, this girl, his child, was disgracing herself and him in the lowest haunts of the city.

"You vile hussy," he cried. "You've no shame in you! You ought to be kicked out into the street, but I'll teach you a lesson that you'll never forget."

The heavy teamster's whip that his son used in driving the great cart horses for the mills was leaning in the corner. Dexter seized it with a nervous clutch. He strode forward and caught the girl again by the wrists.

"We'll see if we can't take a little of the shamelessness out of that pretty skin of yours," he said. "I'd sooner see you dead than have you go on like this. *You*, my daughter! You're worse than the vilest dog in the streets, and I'll show you how I treat such as you."

He raised the heavy whip, but now the girl faced him. Her head was up. The violet eyes flashed with indignation, and her cheeks were scarlet with anger. With a sudden twist of his wiry arm, he threw her down, and the lash descended. At first she lay silent under the blows, biting her soft lip till it bled, then a low moan escaped her and then a scream. Still the blows fell, and it was not till she lay, white and half unconscious that he desisted.

"There," he said, beginning to feel some compunction. "That'll teach you a lesson. From now on I mean you to be a decent girl."

He left the mother to care for her and put her to bed. But Gertrude was silent, and there was a strained, far-away look in her eyes. She made no response to her mother's awkward caresses.

When they looked for her in the morning, she was gone. They searched the house; they visited the neighbours; they patrolled the Bowery; they notified the Police — but they never found her again. To the Lady of Good Cheer, it was a terrible blow, and she never ceased to feel the sadness and horror of it. Often she would stop in her work to wonder what had become of this beautiful child, who in the midst of her drudgery had sought a little of that pleasure which is the rightful portion of every girl, and who had sunk suddenly out of sight in the black bottomless whirlpool of the great city's life, without so much as a ripple to mark where she had disappeared.

Dexter never recovered from the blow. At last his debts were paid. His house was pleasant and comfortable once more. His faith in his wife had not been misplaced. Thanks to the Lady of Good Cheer the long terrible struggle had not been in vain. For it had been her faith that had kept his wife from sinking back into the old slough, and that had nerved him through all the days of bitter toil, when he had felt almost too weak to stand. He had won,—but he had lost his child.

Many months later the minister was standing on the corner of 59th Street waiting for a car, when a tall graceful lady accosted him. She was stylishly dressed, and there was something strangely familiar in the piquant little nose and violet eyes that looked out at him from under the shadow of the large plumed hat.

"Don't you know me?" she asked.

It came over him suddenly.

"Gertrude Dexter!" he cried. "Where have you been, and what are you doing now?"

"Oh, I'm all right," she said. "I'm married

to a fine man, and we live uptown in our own little apartment, and I'm as happy as can be."

"Tell me where you are," he said. "Your father and mother are broken-hearted for loss of you."

She tapped her dainty high-heeled shoe with her parasol nervously.

"No," she said, "I never want to see them or hear of them again," and she turned swiftly and was lost in the crowd.

XXII

THE CURRICULUM OF CITY LIFE

"WAS little Peter Mercer in the yard with the boys this afternoon?" asked the Lady of Good Cheer of the sexton. It was the boys' afternoon in the church yard, which had been turned into an extempore gymnasium, and quite a horde of them had just departed after performing a variety of bewildering antics on the swings and trapeze and bars.

"Peter Mercer?" said the sexton. "I'm not sure as I'm onto his shape. There was enough of them Hamilton Street kids here. Say, them little jiggers is somethin' fierce. One o' them little angels o' yours made me laugh till I near split. Like as not it was Peter."

He pushed his hat back on his brow, and scratched his head as a suppressed grin spread slowly from ear to ear.

"Why, what did he do?" asked the Lady of Good Cheer. "He's a dear little fellow, if it was Peter, but he *is* rather funny."

"Sure he's a dear, all right," said the sexton, the grin spreading a little, "one o' these here mamma's-darlin', Sunday-School angels, ain't he?"

The Lady of Good Cheer smiled. "Well, not exactly that, but I think the world of Peter. What did he do?"

"It ain't what he did, so much as what he didn't do, and what he said," answered the sexton.

When she asked her first question, the Lady of Good Cheer had her hand on the door, just ready to spring out to her work, her slender figure was alive with energy and her lips were compressed with the determination to get through her twenty calls that afternoon late as it was. But something about the twinkle in the sexton's eye detained her. She let the door swing to, and faced around.

"What was it? What did he say?" she asked with some curiosity.

"If I was to tell you all the things them Hamilton kids says in the yard of an afternoon, I'd get the sack for sure," he said.

"Oh, I know them well enough. You needn't be afraid of me," said the Lady of Good Cheer.

"Well," said the sexton, "I was goin' through the yard with a hod o' bricks, that the minister wanted up in the pulpit for one o' these object talks he's a going to give. And one o' them little kids comes runnin' up with his bare feet,— a little kid about eight years old, he was,— and he says, 'Say, Mr. Rainey, whatcher goin' ter do wid them bricks. Goin' ter build a new church?' Well, I turns round a bit to look at him, and when I turns a brick on top o' the hod slips off, and by bad luck it fell down right on the little kid's bare toe. It ain't no joke to have a sharp brick fall on your toe even when you have a boot on, an' thinks I, 'I've paralysed the kid for sure this time,' and I was fer runnin' in to get the nurse to come and hold his hand, an' 'wipe away them tears,' as the sayin' is, but the little kid he picks up his toe all bloody from the brick in one hand, and comes hoppin' up on one foot, an' he give me such a look,—like I was made o' dirt,—an' says he: 'You'd make a hell of a hod carrier, you would!' Laugh! well say, it near killed me, but I didn't want to laugh out loud at the kid, so I near bust. He's got sand, all right. No one is goin' to be pityin' him. It's me that's deservin' his pity fer me ignorance!"

The Lady of Good Cheer threw back her head and laughed lightly with an appreciation of the scene which her mental image of little Peter only made more delicious. "It surely was Peter," she said. "That's just the kind of boy he is. I must run down and see his father. It is time now for him to come home from work."

A few minutes later she was climbing the top flight of stairs in a crowded Hamilton Street tenement. The door of one apartment at the back was open, and within she could see a man down on his knees energetically scrubbing the floor while a sauce pan simmered on the stove. What seemed an unlimited supply of children were huddled about in various corners, leaving the man a free sweep of the floor. He rose as she entered. He was a slim, wiry Cockney with a thin bronzed face, smooth shaven, with black hair and dark eyes. He looked more like a waiter in some uptown club than a fourth ward workingman. He was in his shirt sleeves and his arms were bared and deep in soap suds.

"Beg pardon, Mum, for looking like I do," he said. "But I'm just 'ome from work and I 'aven't 'ad no time to put the 'ouse to rights. I've just started in to scrub up and get the supper, and I 'aven't 'ad no chance to wash the children. Look at 'em! They'll be the death of me. What do you think that boy has been up to now?"

He pointed to a small boy of about eight whose anatomy was concealed in a pair of trousers of truly gigantic proportions. The Lady of Good Cheer saw at once that the father had cut off a few feet of his own trousers and arrayed his son therein. They came up nearly to his shoulders, and his little brown feet protruded from their ragged bottoms. His face was thin and old. There was a weird expression in the wizened little countenance with its funny wrinkles around the mouth. But if the face seemed old it was not reposeful. A pair of narrow black eyes sharp as those of a ferret, were looking at the Lady of Good Cheer from beneath a puckered little brow, with such intense inquisitiveness that she looked away with an uncomfortable feeling. It was as if some uncanny sprite had taken possession of the little body, and were waiting its chance to entrap her and laugh at her behind her back.

The destiny of the family was hanging in the balance, and she knew that this little imp might easily precipitate it into irremediable ruin. He had a right to his eccentricities, for he was that much suspected and maligned person, " the son of a sea-cook." When the Lady of Good Cheer first knew him, Mercer was cook on a steamer. At that time he assumed little responsibility for his family beyond turning over a small portion of his pay to his wife when he returned from his cruises. The rest he expended on the alcoholic stimulus which he felt to be essential in preserving an optimistic outlook on life. The sudden death of his wife had given the Lady of Good Cheer an opportunity to converse with him as to the responsibilities of a father, and the necessity of turning over a new leaf. He responded heartily, by being ashamed of his past behaviour and quite overwhelmed at the thought of the five helpless urchins who owed their existence to him; and he promised to realise as far as possible such hazy ideals of the Pater Familias as hovered in his mind. He gave up his position at once, and got a place in the fish market, so that he could return to the children every evening. He cooked their breakfast every morning, left them something to eat, and went off to work hard all day. He returned at six, scrubbed up the house, got the supper, washed the children, mended their clothes and performed the various duties of an efficient housewife. The house was as neat and clean as a ship's deck, and he had kept everything in such fine shape that the Lady of Good Cheer rejoiced every time she called. It seemed almost too good to last. For a man to work hard all day and then to do the housework for a family of five children seemed almost too great a strain for the masculine mind. Certainly Mercer would have fallen from grace long before but for the visits of the Lady of Good Cheer. When a man plays the martyr so consistently, he requires some audience to applaud and appreciate, and the continued friendship and enthusiastic approval of the Lady of Good Cheer had been enough so far to nerve him to his task. The approval even of one person means much, and if our vast centres of population could ever be organised so that each stray individual would have one friend vitally interested in his success and progress, the frightful degeneration which is the result of the present conditions of social isolation might be successfully checked.

"What is the matter now?" asked the Lady of Good Cheer, taking her stand on an island in the swimming floor and surveying him with a sympathetic glance of humorous despair.

"I don't know what to do with the kids," said Mercer, shaking the suds from his hands in a gesture of despondency. "First I locked them in when I went to work in the morning, and let them out at night when I got back. And then I read as how a tenement near by here was burnt up, an' I thought it would never do to lock them up like that. Mamie there is twelve now, an' she'd orter be able to look after 'em, so this mornin' I told her to mind the house and not let any one in. But what does the girl do but run off to talk with some of the loafers on the street? When she was gone, Peter didn't stay long cooped up, you can bet!

"I was down to the docks lookin' up some fish as was comin' in, an' I 'eard some kind of a row goin' on, an' found a big crowd down on one o' the wharves, sayin' as 'ow a 'orse fell off into the river. They couldn't find 'im or get 'im out, an' I 'eard 'em callin', 'Go it little 'un, that's the stuff!' an' I saw a little kid had chucked off 'is coat an' was divin' in right under the wharf. Pretty soon out he comes with the end of a line. ''Ere he is!' he says. 'Pull on this!' an' by — savin' your prisence,— it was Peter! The current 'ad carried the 'orse down under the wharf an' there he stuck, an' Peter goes divin' in like a little rat an' gets the rein. An' they pulled the 'orse out with him sittin' on its 'ead. Well, I didn't know whether to give 'im a thrashin' or what, but the crowd give 'im a big cheer, an' some one says: 'The kid should git a medal fer life savin'!' 'Sure,' says another, 'he saved a horse, an' most o' them 'eroes don't save nothin' but a blamed ass!' I'm not sayin' it wasn't plucky, but what can a man do with a houseful o' kids like that? Livin' in this 'ere city, it seems like they grow old so fast while yer back's turned, that ye don't know whether you'll find 'em heroes or jailbirds."

A CRIMINAL BY NECESSITY

I

"THE families in this house is all Sheenies and Eyetalians, all but one, and they,—well, they're Irish Jews!" said the housekeeper with a furtive grin.

"Irish Jews!" exclaimed the Lady of Good Cheer, "that is something new in the ward. I've met Japanese and Russians, and Finns and Letts and Lithuanians and Greeks, but I've never seen an Irish Jew."

"It's a bit like mixin' water and oil, ain't it?" responded the janitor. "They say Pat Moriarty, the feller that cut up such a row in the ward and was mixed up in the stabbing affair over to Tim Flannery's,—well, they say Pat says to his wife one day, says he, 'When I kick up me heels, mind you take and bury me over to the Sheeny Cemetury in Chatham Square.' An' says she, rollin' her eyes in horror: 'What for would I be puttin' the bones of a good Irishman from County Cork among all them Jews?' An' says he, wid a twinkle in his eye, 'Put me there, Kate; put me there. Sure, 'tis the last place the divil will be lookin' for me.'"

The tale was one in which the ward delighted, and the grin on the janitor's countenance was so irresistible that the Lady of Good Cheer laughed as spontaneously as if the denouement had been unexpected. No strangers who saw her in her trim winter suit of soft brown, that harmonised so delightfully with the tint of her hair and gave such an air of youth to her energetic figure, would have suspected her of being anything akin to that highly virtuous but occasionally unpopular slum angel, the "missionary lady." Generations of Puritan ancestors had indeed bestowed upon her a mouth straight and firm, an aquiline nose and a strong chin not to be trifled with. These determined features were forgotten however, because of her eyes,— eyes which Botticelli might have painted in some St. Elizabeth who had seen much of life's struggle and pondered long on human weakness, and which yet had not lost that mischievous glint that so often makes strangers kin. They were twinkling now as she answered the janitor.

"I imagine Pat is safe. I, for one, shan't look for him there, and I don't think I shall climb many stairs looking for a family of Irish Jews."

"I'm tellin' ye straight; they're Irish Jews all right," said the janitor, aggrieved at her lack of faith, "and say," he came a step nearer and spoke mysteriously, "I wouldn't wonder if they had some reason for dodging the divil. There's somethin' mighty queer about 'em. The man's a cock-eyed little bantam, and I'll bet me hat he ain't on the level. He hits the pipe or plays the ponies or tips off some gang o' crooks,— you take it from me, he's up to something. Go up and see fer yourself. They've got a lot o' kids fer your Sunday School. They're on the third floor, front, left."

The lady was anxious to learn if such an incredible compound of nation and creed had in truth been precipitated in this strange laboratory of human nature. She set off at once with swift steps to explore. She had been standing in the dark hall of the front house while she conversed with the janitor, who was going through certain motions which would lead the world to suppose he was scrubbing down the stairs. She went out the back door, crossed the narrow stone-paved court, and began to run lightly up the worn steps of the rear house, whistling a snatch of song as she went. She knocked at the door indicated by the janitor, and a voice called "Come in!" It was an unusually sweet and pleasant voice, very different from the strident and raucous tones of foreign accent that usually saluted the ears in the fourth ward, and she was at once interested in its owner. She opened the door upon the usual two-room apartment, with its bare floors, stove, kitchen table, a few wooden chairs, and, in the room beyond, a bed. There was little enough, but it is surprising out of what rudimentary materials the hand of genius can create a home. It was evident that such a hand was here. Even without the cleverly arranged flowers and coloured prints, the room with its smooth white floors and shining table and gleaming dishes was bright enough in itself, a true little temple of the Lares and Penates, upon whose black polished altar, the kitchen stove, the fire was always burning and a sweet incense ascending to the nostrils of gods and men.

In the room were two little girls of ten and twelve. The elder had a thin, elfish face and sharp little eyes that peered out under a tangle of dark hair. Her features were regular and delicate, and showed possibilities of beauty. The other girl had a typical Irish face, blue eyes and brown hair, a little snub nose, a saucy mouth and a dimpled chin. A handsome little brown-eyed boy played on the floor. But the attention of the Lady of Good Cheer was absorbed by a woman who sat in the rocking-chair holding a baby in her arms. There was something peculiarly sweet and madonna-like in her features and attitude. Her colouring and the outline of her face suggested an old Murillo altar piece; but with all its sweetness, there was a firmness about the delicate lips, and a strength in the chin that one does not find in the Spanish master. The eyes, too, belonged to a different school. Large and lustrous, now grey and now blue in the changing light, they seemed to render the whole face strangely luminous.

"I came to ask if you would like to send your children to Sunday School, Mrs. Donovan," said the Lady of Good Cheer, after the preliminaries of greeting.

"I don't know. You'll have to ask my husband. He was bound Annie and Sallie should go to the parochial school. I'd as soon they'd go to the public school myself. I was brought up a Jewess, you see, but my husband's a Catholic, and when he was married I told him he could send the children to the Catholic School. And now he's got his way, manlike, he don't seem to like it," she went on, her face lighting up with a smile. It was not that familiar, cynical smile of the wife, but rather the tolerant and sympathetic smile of the mother. Here, then, was the explanation of that anomaly, the Irish Jew. An Irishman had defied the traditions of his church and family, and had married a Jewess. But this apparently was not all. The Lady of Good Cheer was conscious of some further mystery in the background as Mrs. Donovan continued.

"He says the girls don't learn a thing. He'd be pitching into the sisters and priests from morning to night, if I'd let him. I'm afraid he isn't a very good Catholic."

The smile was gone now, and something like a sigh escaped her lips.

"I should like so much to meet him and have a talk some day. Do you think he'd pitch into me?" asked the Lady of Good Cheer, with a smile.

"I wish you could talk to him." Mrs. Donovan had grown suddenly serious. Unsuspected lines of anxiety appeared in her smooth brow, and a mist seemed to gather over her eyes, causing them to change as a mountain pool changes under the shadow of a cloud from grey green to a greyer blue. She must have been damming up a great flood of anxiety for months, and the sympathetic note in the voice of the Lady of Good Cheer had suddenly loosed the gates.

"I'm so troubled about him I don't know what to do. I came on here hoping things would be better, and they're worse than ever. I don't know what will become of us! I haven't a friend in the city!"

The Lady of Good Cheer reached out instinctively and took her hand.

"Can I help any?" she asked. "Won't you tell me about it?"

Her eyes spoke more eloquently than her voice, and Mrs. Donovan looked into them gratefully a moment. Then she shook her head, and bravely repressed the tears, and said: "No, I can't tell you. You must ask him. He'll be honest with you, I know. Can't you wait? He ought to be coming in now."

She spoke truly. They had waited but a few minutes when the door opened and Donovan appeared. Slight and delicate of form he was, but he had an individuality that would have drawn attention anywhere. He gazed in surprise at the Lady of Good Cheer, his small round head cocked a little on one side, his mouth open, his parted lips revealing his uneven and broken teeth beneath the heavy black moustache that drooped to conceal them. His eyes were pale and weak, and as he surveyed the Lady of Good Cheer, they twitched continually and shifted from side to side. But with all these physical disadvantages there was something very attractive about the little man. It was a certain Celtic vivacity, combined with a most unusual straightforwardness and directness, that gave a distinct charm to all he said. His hands were as delicate as a girl's, and evidently incapable of hard labour. Mrs. Donovan started to introduce him, but Donovan waved her aside.

"How d'ye do, ma'am," he said. "I've seen you at the meeting up to the church. I've been in once or twice with a pal o' mine. I like to drop in where there's good singin'. My friend was scared the roof would fall in on him, it bein' a Protestant Church; but I'm no bigot, if I am a Catholic."

"I remember seeing you, and I heard you, too," said the Lady of Good Cheer. "You have a good tenor voice. You must come regularly and help with the singing, if you aren't going anywhere else."

"No," he said with sudden fierceness, "the church ain't no place fer me."

He broke off abruptly and added apologetically, "Not that the church ain't all right in its way, ye understand. But I've no use for priests and clergymen. We don't hit it off, as ye might say. I might come in now and then and hear the singin' though. Little Johnny likes singin' too. He can sing 'Sweet Peace' as well as his dad, can't ye Johnny?"

And he picked the three-year-old boy up in his arms and began crooning a song a line at a time, while the little baby voice lisped it after him in broken childish accent, but with remarkable accuracy of note.

"There, now!" he said, laughing, and tossing the boy in his arms. "What do you think of that?"

"He sits by the hour with that boy on his knee, singing the songs over and over," said his wife.

"Johnny is going to make a singer, surely," said the Lady of Good Cheer. "I wish you would send the children up to Sunday School, and we will teach them all the songs."

"Sure, I believe in sendin' children to school," said Donovan. "But here in New York the schools ain't no good. Them two girls don't learn a thing. Up in Boston, where I was brought up, they have decent schools, and the children knew something; but here in New York there ain't no education at all. They're the most ignorant lot I ever saw."

"We should be glad to have your children in our schools, but if you are really Catholics, we don't want you to leave your own church," said the Lady of Good Cheer.

"I'm not much of a Catholic," said Donovan. "'Tain't no fault of me mother's, neither. If the Catholic religion could ever have percolated me obstinate hide, me mother would have druv it through with her old brogan. When I'd ask her to send me to the public school, she'd tell me the priest knew more than George Washington and Abraham Lincoln rolled into one. I must respect the priests, like I did the holy saints or Tim Lonergan, the ward boss, ye know. Well, I was a wild young kid, and the pleasures of high thinkin' and pious livin', such as Father McGinnis give us at the parochial school, was about as tasty to me as cornstarch and water, when I could skip off and get a seat in the Nigger Heaven at the Howard, and I played hookey till one day me mother sent the priest after me. Well, when he caught me and began handin' out enough of this here virtuous talk to fill a phonograph, about me bein' an idler and reprobate, I got red-headed. When I get mad I don't know what I'm doin', and that day I was crazy. I called him all the names,— well, I tell you, I give him a reg'lar evolutionary peddygree, callin' him the son of pretty near everything from an angleworm down. But he didn't take no stock in Darwin, and perhaps I did give his ansisterial tree an extra limb or two, like guns and seacooks, which them professors don't recognise as bein' in the straight line.

"Anyhow, he caught hold of me, and tried to shut off the flow of me jeaneological reminiscences. The minute he put his hand to me, I went clean off me nut and grabbed up a stick and hit him with all me might and ran fer it. He come around to the house, and told me mother he wasn't angry but terrible grieved. Grieved! I didn't know much, but I knew that ain't no fit word to describe a man's feelin's when he gets a crack on the crazy bone with the edge of a fence-rail, and I skipped out. Me mother gave me up entirely from that day. She said I was under the curse of God. I'd insulted a priest, and no good would come of me. That's how me contryversy with the church begun, and we ain't hit it off no better since. The priest had it in for me and no wonder, and I'd get mad and answer back every time they tackled me. So all me folks in Boston, bein' good Catholics, look on me with holy horror, and call me a renegade and a crook. But they're none too good themselves fer all their religion. 'Twas they started me on the booze. The can was always going in our house. If they'd sent me to a good trade school instead of botherin' me with religion, I'd be all right now."

The Lady of Good Cheer had listened, fascinated by the torrent of speech that poured forth from the little man, as he sat on the edge of his chair accentuating his words by an impetuous wave of his slim white hand. She broke in at this point.

"What work do you find here in New York to do?" she asked. He looked at her a moment in silence, his head on one side like a suspicious ferret, his pale eyes twitching and shifting, his parted lips showing the uneven teeth. Then he seemed to stiffen suddenly, and with an almost savage defiance he spoke at last.

"I'm a professional gambler, that's what I am!" He flung the words out as a knight might have flung his gauntlet in his enemy's teeth. The Lady of Good Cheer suppressed a start of surprise. She realised that her future relations with this family depended on the way in which she received this challenge.

"I don't know much about that kind of work," she said as calmly, as if he had stated that he was a professor of Biblical Archeology. "I've heard it criticised by people who knew little of it. What do you think of it yourself? Is it all right?"

It was a confidential appeal which would have touched the honour of any professional man. In spite of her assumed nonchalance she watched him with almost trembling interest. He gave her a puzzled look, and when he spoke his voice was no longer defiant.

"Sometimes it's honest, and some men play on the level." He paused a moment and then added sullenly: "But I don't. I'm a professional card cheat."

Again he looked at her, as if he expected an outburst; but finding only a look of sympathetic interest, he went on:

"I know every trick in the trade. I can deal four aces to myself and my partners every time. I always play on the square with my friends, and they know that. Jerry would rather cut off his hand than do them dirty, but when any of these fool loafers come in trying to skin everybody, why, we just get up a little game, and I can carry off the boodle. I play the piano down to O'Rourke's place, you see, and I pick up a game or two every evening."

"O'Rourke's?" said the Lady of Good Cheer interrogatively.

"Yes, he's got a pool room back of his saloon in Catherine Street, and I play the piano and jolly the boys a bit every evening."

"Do you like it? Do you want to keep on making money that way?"

Mrs. Donovan let the sewing she had taken up drop from her hands, and looked over at her husband, while the anxious lines gathered again on her brow.

"Like it? No!" he cried. "I'm ashamed of myself. I want to be on the level." He jumped to his feet and began walking up and down the room with the restlessness of a caged fox.

"What can I do with a wife and four children? I'm not strong enough for heavy work, and my eyes are too bad to do writing. I can't live honest if I try. It's no use!"

There was something in the accents of those words, "It's no use," that told of hard effort and cruel disappointment. They were not the usual flippant excuse of the criminal who "could not help it." Yet the Lady of Good Cheer felt them to be absurd. To state that there is no way in which a man possessed of all his limbs and senses can keep his family from starvation, save by card-cheating, seemed ridiculous, and she challenged the remark at once.

"You say it's no use trying to be honest," she said, "and I see you believe it. But I don't," she went on with a smile, "and I think down at the bottom you know that, when a man follows the right as he sees it, no matter what it costs, God will take care of that man. Why don't you try it? Certainly you can't be much worse off than you are now, for I know you are unhappy. No man is so miserable as one who is doing every day what he feels is wrong. And it will only grow harder. How will it be when that little boy grows up? What will he think of his father? Oh, Mr. Donovan, do give it up, and if there is anything I can do to help you, I'll do it."

While she had been leading him on to speak of himself, her face had been to him as a dark house-front, with curtained windows and unknown interior, from which came only a voice. Now suddenly every window blazed with light. Even his dull twitching eye saw something of the character within as the shutters opened. He looked at her a few moments in vague surprise. His wife watched his face intently, clasping and unclasping her tense fingers and winking away the tears that one by one clouded her clear grey eyes.

"Well," he said at last. "I'll try it. I believe in God, ye understand, and I know what's right. I was brought up in Boston, and I'm an honest man at heart. It'll make my wife happy if I cut out the cards,—eh, Meg?" And he reached over and patted his wife's cheek. "She's a good wife if there ever was one," he added.

Her cheeks were still wet, but she looked up at the strange little man with a tender smile, that seemed full of sacred utterances, and she touched his hand shyly.

"Oh, Jerry! I'm so glad!" she said softly, "and I'll help too."

"I'll bet you, you will," he said affectionately throwing his arm around her. "She's a good woman, and she's always stuck by me even when I treated her mean. Her own folks cut her off because she stood up for me."

He looked at her no longer ashamed and despairing, but filled with that inflating pride which is the last support of many a man despised by the world, who knows there is one woman still to whom he is of supreme importance, and who will give up the whole world for his sake. And with a proud laugh he said: "You'll never go back on your old Jerry, will you?"

II

It was some months later that the Lady of Good Cheer was running up the stairway to Donovan's rooms with hurried and anxious steps. Donovan had received a summons to appear in court that day, and had promised to be at the church early in the morning to make arrangements for the trial, but he had not appeared. The little gambler had certainly been put to a severe test. He had given up his place in the poolroom and sought for work. There were thousands unemployed that winter, and he would have failed but for a succession of great snowstorms that clogged the thoroughfares and compelled the street-cleaning department to call for hundreds of extra men. Donovan volunteered, and night after night took his stand in the great square on East Broadway, his slight little figure almost indistinguishable in the long line of hulking Irishmen and stout Germans. By the light of the flaring torches he struggled with a huge snow shovel, trying to lift load after load of wet, soggy snow into the carts that came along in unending lines. He was up to his knees in slush, and soaked through with the melting snow which ran up his sleeves and down his back. Every muscle ached with the unaccustomed toil, and many times he sank down exhausted on the wet snow bank. The stronger men, used to ditch-digging and hard labour, looked at him in pity.

"You ain't fit for this job, me boy. You'd best chuck it. Stop your diggin', or they'll be diggin' you a hole six feet by two in a day or so."

But Donovan thought of the hungry mouths at home, and picked up his shovel.

"Thanks, but I'll stick to me job. There's a way to make both ends meet without workin', but its debilitatin' to the moral backbone, as the snake said, when he began to swallow his tail," he said cheerily, splashing and staggering through the slush with his heavily loaded shovel.

"Say, you can't heave that into the cart. Get along! You're in the way," said another big fellow.

"I'm lookin' fer a job to lecture on Woman's Rights and Men's Wrongs at a hundred per, but till I land it, I'm goin' to stick to me snow shovel, you can bet!" he answered.

So he held his own through the long hours of night, and at last in the icy grey dawn he staggered home, his soaked garments frozen stiff, every muscle aching and his whole body exhausted. So it went on night after night. Hiding his growing weakness under a mask of absurd banter, he drove his frail, exhausted body back to the toil, and kept it somehow at work by sheer force of will, until one day he found himself unable to rise from bed, his head throbbing and fever burning in every vein.

"I ain't fakin', this ain't no attack o' neurosterics," he said to the Lady of Good Cheer when she called, "but you see it ain't no use. I can't keep up with a row of donkey engines like them fellers. If snow shovels was worked by the jaw, I'd have them big Dutchies on the run to keep up with me, though."

Mrs. Donovan took hold during his sickness, and did her utmost to support the family. In the early mornings and evenings she scrubbed out the dirty floors of a big office building, till her hands were blistered and chapped with the hard toil and icy water. Her steps were slow as she made her way down town in the freezing grey dawn, for in a few weeks her little baby would be born, and many a time as she knelt on the cold marble floors, scrubbing with might and main, she thought she would faint from the terrible pangs of pain that shot through her. But she always returned to her husband, with some joke about her growing acquaintance with the plutocrats and her success as a practical muckraker in Wall Street, and hid her bleeding hands from his sight. She worked up to within a day or two of the child's birth, and then she too gave out, and lay helpless in her bed. They could not afford a doctor, and were too proud to be charity patients. They did not tell the Lady of Good Cheer of their needs, but called in a Jewish midwife who brought Mrs. Donovan safely through the ordeal.

When he recovered, Donovan could find no work, and Mrs. Donovan was too weak to take up her scrubbing. It is needless to dwell on those weeks of anxiety, when the cries of their hungry children made them nearly desperate. Many a basket did the Lady of Good Cheer send in to keep the wolf from the door. But there was that ever present bugbear, more persistent and voracious in modern cities than the traditional wolf,—the rent. Donovan counted every spare penny, and found himself two months behind. They had agreed to give the midwife three dollars, and when they failed to pay after repeated dunning, she brought suit for ten dollars. This was the last straw, and Donovan, who had met his disasters with so cheery a fund of banter, sank beneath it.

The Lady of Good Cheer had asked the minister to go with Donovan to the court and speak for him, but Donovan had not appeared at the church, and it was with a fear of some impending disaster that she hurried up the narrow stair of the tenement. A feeble voice called " Come in," and she threw open the door and could not restrain a cry of amazement and horror. The pretty little room was a chaos of confusion and dirt. The chairs were overturned, broken crockery and smashed flower pots lay on the floor, with the earth strewn everywhere. Huddled in a chair, a pitiful figure, sat Donovan, his moustache drooping, his lips parted in a forlorn snarl, which bared his blackened uneven teeth. He looked like some hunted animal, harassed by dogs and at bay. His shifty eyes twitched violently, and he looked up in a dazed way, blinking at the Lady of Good Cheer. On the bed in the room beyond lay Mrs. Donovan, sobbing.

"Oh, Mr. Donovan!" she cried. "What has happened!"

He said nothing, but continued to look at her with dazed, twitching eyes. She went into the bedroom, and sat down by the sick woman, who lay weeping with the tiny red-faced morsel of flesh beside her.

The Lady of Good Cheer took her hand gently, and said: "How can I help you? Don't be afraid to tell me all about it."

Brokenly she told what had happened. It would have seemed a work of witchcraft were it not so common. The marvel was not that her husband's courage should have broken at last under the steady hammering of adverse fate. The strange thing was that the personality of the man with his frankness and tenderness and humour, should have totally disappeared from its habitation and vanished into space, at the touch upon his brain of the fiery fumes of the stimulant to which he had turned in his despair; while in its place, a malicious demon, as false as it was cruel, had usurped his body, heaped curses and blows on the woman he loved best, and sought to shatter to pieces the pretty little home he had worked so hard to maintain. We may never know enough of personality to fathom this mystery, and yet we are willing to treat it as a vulgar commonplace. Mrs. Donovan said that for many years these turns had come periodically. Once in so often the madness seized him, and nothing could be done till it was over. She had been told it was hopeless to cure him, but he had not touched alcohol since giving his word to the Lady of Good Cheer until now. There was little time to lose. The Lady of Good Cheer did what she could to restore him to a right mind, and in some measure succeeded. It was, however, but a wretched, bedraggled specimen of humanity that accompanied the minister to the court some time later.

The Civil Court is a shade more respectable and agreeable than the Police Court. It seems little enough like America, for it is always crowded with Russian Jews, who with their endless petty suits are always working the ropes of American justice with the excited eagerness of children who have just moved into a house with an elevator, and who like to see the wheels go round. It was filled now with a vociferous group, who were clamouring over some suit as to their synagogue taxes, each side with fifteen or twenty witnesses from whom the very smooth young lawyers were trying to extract some coherent statement, while the judge sat immovable behind the barriers on his varnished throne, scribbling notes and occasionally casting a bored glance at the contestants over his glasses. As soon as the last lawyer finished his eloquent peroration, the judge addressed a few remarks to a spot on the ceiling in the polite tone of a man who is giving his wife the same advice for the fiftieth time, and in a second the officers were bundling the excited litigants out of the court in a mad whirl of gabbling gesticulation.

In another second the case of Rebecca Goldstein vs. Jerry Donovan had been called. The young Jew who represented the midwife, after exhibiting some reams of elegant phraseology recently acquired at the City College, called on half a score of excited Hebrew dames in shawl and scheitel to substantiate his statements. The judge called Donovan, and as he stood up bedraggled and shaking, his Honour eyed him over the top of his glasses with the misanthropic glance of one confirmed in his opinion that all flesh is something even less intelligent than grass.

"Anything to say for yourself?" he enquired.

Donovan stood with twitching eyes, speechless for once. In his part of the worthy and injured father of a family, he appealed to the risibilities of the spectators rather than to their sympathies. The minister was embarrassed. He could answer the lawyer's arguments easily, but Donovan himself was an argument before which he was helpless. The more earnestly he spoke, the more patent grew the grin with which the crowd surveyed the bewildered defendant. He spoke for the wife, told of the midwife's inadequate attentions, and ended with as pathetic an appeal as he could make.

"After she had agreed on three dollars," he said, "she has the face to ask of this poor woman, who has toiled till she is sick to pay her bills, the sum of ten dollars, which is double the customary amount, as you know."

The judge, who had apparently been absorbed in philosophic contemplation, suddenly came to life. He dropped his pencil and looked the minister full in the face with a withering glance of offended dignity.

"As I know!" he burst out with a sudden explosion of wrath, that echoed through the court room till even the loafers asleep by the door looked up,—"I'm not married! How on earth should I know the customary prices of midwives?"

The clerk smiled voluminously, the lawyers laughed, the officers burst into a roar which the loafers echoed vociferously. The minister started to turn away in disgust, thinking the day lost, but the judge was at last in better humour. He pounded for order, and his face relaxed into a half smile.

"Five dollars and costs," he said.

This was far better than the minister had feared. He paid the bill and departed with Donovan tagging along, silent and dejected like a whipped dog.

It is needless to recapitulate the trying days that followed for the Lady of Good Cheer, till Donovan was himself again. Wherever it came from, the spirit that possessed him was no more like Donovan than a jelly fish is like a sea urchin. Instead of the straightforward, pugnacious honesty which was his chief characteristic, she was met by shifty deception and even direct lies and fits of furious temper alternated with deep dejection. She was sure, however, that the old Donovan was still somewhere in the universe and made her preparations with a sure faith in his return. By telling his story to a kindly employer, she secured a position for him as porter in a large dry-goods store, and when the real Donovan returned once more, he entered upon his new job with enthusiasm.

III

"CAN'T you find some clothes up to the church to fit out this fellow here?" said Donovan to the Lady of Good Cheer. She had dropped into his house at supper time, and to her amazement found a stranger, an exceedingly ragged young man, seated at the table between Mrs. Donovan and Annie. There was nothing left of his boots but a few pieces of leather and his ragged, dirty coat was buttoned to the throat to conceal the lack of a shirt. He was over six feet tall and his trousers, even at their best, were totally inadequate to cover his spacious outlines. They came but little below the knee, and his strenuous but futile efforts to increase their circumference in the equatorial zone had resulted only in gaping disaster. His face was covered with stubble, and his brow and neck with a long tangle of black hair, but beneath this guise it was possible to discern a frank manly face.

"I stopped in to see the boys at O'Rourke's," went on Donovan, "and I found him sittin' in the back room. It was rainin', and he'd come in to get dry. He hadn't a cent to buy drink, and he ain't a drinkin' man, anyway. He hadn't had a bite to eat all day, and hadn't located no place where he could sleep,— not so much as an old barrel. I see he was a decent young feller, and I says: 'Come along, Tom, me boy; come up to my house, and I'll give you a bite to eat and a place to sleep till ye land a job. I know what hard luck is meself.' He's got a fine bass voice, and if you'll fit him out, I'll bring him up to the Men's Club to sing in the quartette."

The Lady of Good Cheer was somewhat nonplussed by this announcement. Donovan was hardly in a position to be supplying stray men with board and lodging. He had made a desperate effort to fill efficiently the position she had found for him, but in an institution which affords such diversities of employment as the modern department store, there seemed to be no hole of opportunity adjusted to fit a peg of such eccentric shape. He could not handle heavy cases, and they set him to clean windows; but when he was once balanced in the air outside a fifth story window, his brains were reduced to such a vertiginous state that he had to be pulled in. Inability to perform delicate gymnastics on a narrow ledge sixty feet above a stone pavement is not necessarily proof of moral obliquity or even of industrial incapacity, and Donovan might have escaped a discharge, but for the fact that he was handicapped still farther by an inherent inability to restrain unuttered any thought generated by his highly effervescent brain cells. Dante applied the heaviest kind of punishment to the most consummate hypocrite, but in common experience the man of perfect frankness is the one who receives it. It chanced that one of the floor-walkers, who belonged to the church, failed to recognise Donovan, who supposed that this was an intentional slight put upon him because of his prior occupation, and it roused his sensitive soul to such a pitch of indignant fury that when he was summoned and reprimanded for his delinquency in reference to the windows, he burst forth into a truly Demosthenic denunciation of department stores and all their retainers; and the managers, who were not interested in vivid language and highly coloured metaphors, promptly discharged him. During the period of desperate struggle that followed, he regretted his words, of course, but it seemed to him that the managers should have understood that it was "just Jerry Donovan shootin' off his mouth, and no harm meant." At last, by his own effort, he secured a place in a stable in Cherry Street,— not an artistic, aseptic, highly polished stable with brass mountings and hand-embroidered horse-blankets, but a dark, noisome place, Augean in its accumulation of dirt and debris, and located in an ancient building which had long lost its beauty and moral character and which appeared thoroughly decrepit and intoxicated.

The dark jaws of this dank, disreputable edifice swallowed up Jerry every day from six A. M. until nine P. M., so that he saw but little of the sun.

He toiled away in the dim light in air that was dense with strong odours. The work, though not unusually hard, was a Herculean task for Donovan's weak muscles, and when it was over he might be found sitting on a heap of straw and manure in the corner, singing some new street song to a crowd of grinning stablemen. He kept his little " Salon " of the dung heap going, even when, after some months of confinement in such an atmosphere, his health began to fail. His good cheer was not based on the amount of his wages, which seemed far from munificent to one accustomed to feel his pockets stuffed with carelessly crushed, crinkly bills. It barely paid the rent and fed the five little mouths. And lo! here was another capacious mouth which he proposed to feed from the same thinly flowing Pactolean stream. The Lady of Good Cheer rebelled at the folly and sin of it, but her remonstrance died on her lips at his look of amazement.

" Why, ain't that what you was talkin' about up to the church? " he asked; " treatin' poor folks in trouble as if they was your brothers, and takin' 'em in, an' trustin' the Lord to see ye through, when you're doin' the right thing by a poor cuss that's on his uppers? I ain't much of a Christian, but I want to do a bit here and there to help along, ye understand."

The Lady of Good Cheer was fairly beaten, and retired with a quizzical smile at herself for actually having remonstrated with an ex-gambler for being too good a Christian. The immediate result was that Harkins, his protégé, received a suit a little more commensurate with his superficial area, and was escorted by Donovan to the Men's Club, where he sang, "Rocked in the Cradle of the Deep," in a basso profundo that brought down the house.

The Men's Club was nominally a Bible Class, but there were few things in Heaven and earth that were not freely discussed in the course of the evening. On this night some casual allusion was made to the dubious political integrity of a certain henchman of Tammany Hall. Donovan was on his feet in an instant, his head on one side, as he looked at his opponent out of his good eye, like a little bantam about to strike. "You're always givin' Tammany Hall the call down," he said, "but I want ye to understand there ain't a squarer man in New York City than Tom Hennessy, the boss of this here district. Many's the hour I've spent in his poolroom, and when the boys'd get talkin' religion, an' I'd put in me oar and stick up fer this church, they'd all pitch on me and call me a turncoat and a two faced hypocrite and a black Protestant, and tell me to dig out or I'd get me face smashed. An' then Tom would speak up to say, 'Here, you boys, let him alone! He's got as good a right to bark fer his religion as you have.' An' he says to me, 'Jerry, me boy, come in whenever you want. Don't mind them loony geezers. You're always welcome in my saloon. You're one o' these fellers that can't chew yer thoughts in quiet, and swallow down yer feelin's. Ye've got to spit 'em all over town, and I like ye fer it. Ye might have kep' yer mouth shet about your religion in a gang like that, but ye was bound ter stick up fer yer church, if they kicked yer pants off.' An' talk about helpin' the poor! There ain't a poor man in this ward 'as died without a cent to buy crêpe rosettes fer his coffin, but Tom has give him a decent send off, and fixed him up as pretty a little funeral as if he'd been one of the family. An' there ain't a poor soul that's been put out of house and home in this ward these ten years, but Tom has put his hand in his pants and paid the rent, if they was decent deservin' folks and voted the straight ticket. Yes, sir, if you're lookin' fer real Christian gentlemen, Tom Hennessy and the minister's the two finest men in the world."

At this there was an ominous groan, and the Republican district leader slouched out of his chair to his full height of six feet-three, and surveying the little bantam over his broken nose, shook his huge fist and shouted: "D'ye want ter get yer neck broke? If ye don't close yer face, there'll be somethin' comin' your way right now, see? The minister and Tom Hennessy! Did ever any one hear the like?" He turned to the chairman, and continued more calmly: "I don't stand fer all this goo-goo talk about the corruption of Tammany. Ye've got ter divvy the boodle, or you'd have no party. These here dude reformers is wreckin' the Republican Party. When a man has sat up mornin' and night, and worked like a horse, pounding the heads o' these fool Sheenies and Dagoes to make 'em vote the straight ticket, herdin' 'em to the primaries and puttin' the fear o' Gawd in 'em on Election Day so they won't vote both tickets, then, when he's turned out a solid Republican vote of two hundred in a district where there ain't no Republicans at all ter speak of, he goes round thinkin' they'll do the square thing by him, and they politely shows him the door, tellin' him he done it all fer the good o' the city. Do they suppose a poor man with a family o' kids ter feed is goin' ter give up his time and strength, workin' noon and night to hustle up a big vote, when all he gets fer it is a hand out o' pious talk on his self-sacrificin' toil? Tom Rot! Why in the name of mud should a man work like a nigger for his party, if they give all the soft jobs to the Democrats, and tell him to chase himself fer the glory of America? Nixy! The corruption o' Tammany's all very well fer a write up in them dude papers, but Tom Hennessy's a good practical politician, and when a man votes fer him, he sees him through. He's all right that away, I'll allow, but when you talk about Tom Hennessy and the minister, ye make me sick!"

The presiding officer averted a personal conflict by suggesting that if the men down town had as much wealth and leisure as those up town, they might then be willing to work disinterestedly for the good of the city.

This aroused Donovan again, and he sprang to his feet. "That's the trouble with this country!" he shouted. "It's an outrage a few men in Wall Street should have all the money in the land, when there are thousands of poor honest working folks, that can't get enough to keep their children from starving, no matter how hard they try! It's all wrong! It ain't Christian! It ain't justice! All them millions they've squeezed out of the poor ought to be divided up!"

This speech awakened an enthusiastic response from the assembled crowd. There were some seventy men present. For all of them life had been a hard struggle. There had been a period, when they had given up all effort to maintain respectability. Whenever they had had money, they had sought to drown the despair and wretchedness of their lives in intoxication. Since joining the club, however, they had all renounced alcohol, but their families still dreaded the holidays that came after pay day had filled their pockets.

The presiding officer looked over their faces

and said: "Now honestly, suppose it was all divided, and you each got a thousand dollars what would happen?"

There was a moment's pause, then one of them who had been long out of work, and whose family had suffered cruelly from hunger, said: "We'd all be dead or in jail inside a week!"

Donovan's faith in Harkins, his protégé, was not unrewarded. After living some months as Donovan's guest, he at last secured a good position and moved away. When he called a year later, he found his benefactor in disastrous circumstances. A new babe had just been born, and Donovan, sick with the hard labour in the stables and desperately anxious, had again broken out in one of his old time sprees. He lost his job, and Mrs. Donovan was sick and despondent. Harkins, quite overcome at the sight of so much misery, excused himself and quickly withdrew. It took all the patience and genius of the Lady of Good Cheer to get Donovan straightened out again. She made up her mind that severe and radical measures were necessary to save him from himself, and one day he came up to the church and signed with great solemnity a formal *lettre de cachet,* authorising the minister or the Lady of Good Cheer to lock him up at once in jail at the first preliminary sign that he was drinking. It was a most effective pledge. From that day he never drank again. When he felt sure of himself, he joined the church, which he had always refused to do, for fear he might bring disgrace upon an institution he respected. He got back his place at the stable, and as his wife was a genius at housekeeping and had even won a prize for making a dollar go further in purchasing food than any woman in the ward, he managed to get along with his increased family. The family income was eked out by Mrs. Donovan's scrubbing in the office buildings, and by the return of his oldest son, who had spent some years in the Reform School for stealing, and who now found work. It was strange how the family history was written in the faces of the children. This boy, born during the period of their greatest disgrace and disaster, had a misshapen imp-like face, fascinatingly like that of a monkey. His nose was bridgeless, and his mouth wide, with an ever present grin. The three youngest girls, born in the days when hope had revived, were unusually beautiful children and had the mother's regular features and charm.

IV

"It's no use," said Donovan. "I can't be a Christian. It's no use tryin' any more."

The Lady of Good Cheer was sitting in his room and had been imploring him to come back to the church.

"God knows," he said, "I want to be on the level, and I tried me best, but I can't see the kids starve. You folks can be good and do the right thing, but it ain't in the game fer me. There ain't a man on God's earth as wants to do right mor'n I do, but it's no go."

His eyes twitched nervously, and he brushed the back of his hand across them furtively.

"I ain't no hypocrite, anyway," he went on. "When I ain't livin' straight, I won't hang around the church and pretend I'm a good Christian. No, I'm a professional card cheat, that's what I am; and it's no use my tryin' to be no church deacon. I done my best, but I can't get no work on the level that'll keep me and the children."

Donovan had held out bravely at his work in the stable. The months and years had passed, and from six A. M. to nine P. M. he had stuck to his place in the malodorous barracks in Cherry Street. Some days he was sick and could scarcely stand. Still he kept at it, until at last a more serious illness brought him to his bed. This time he permanently lost his position. His wife did her utmost to help out. She took on extra scrubbing, and though another babe was about to be born, she kept to her work, coming home late in the bitter cold, staggering often, with her hands cracked and bleeding, after kneeling an hour or two on the stone floors in the dirty icy water.

It chanced that Tim, the oldest boy, took just this time for a relapse. The few dollars he earned as errand boy was all applied to the rent, much to his disgust, for a boy likes to spend a dime on candy and moving-pictures now and then, and Tim often went hungry. A dollar left on the desk one day offered such irresistible possibilities of enjoyment that Tim's fingers could not refrain from seizing it. He was detected and discharged. His father was so furious that he dared not come home for three nights.

It seemed that his efforts to do right were drawing down upon him a chain of disasters. Annie had grown into a pretty girl of sixteen with a saucy face, and flashing dark eyes under her tangle of brown hair. Mrs. Donovan had to scrub to help with the rent, and the housework fell mainly upon Annie, and she resented it. She had to take care of the baby and scrub out the house and get the meals. She had no time for amusement, and her clothes were ragged. It was not strange that during her parents' absence, she stole out into the street and hung about with the young loafers on the corner for a little fun. Worn out and irritable with hard work, Mrs. Donovan found fault with her, and scolded her again and again. Now there was a new and changed expression in Annie's face. A wild, dare-devil look had come into her eyes. She was rebellious and taciturn, now giving way to furious fits of temper, now moody and silent, and refusing to answer every question. Her mother first discovered the tragedy that lay behind this strange change in the girl. She dared not tell Donovan, and it was long before he discovered that his daughter was disgraced in the eyes of the world. Donovan's affection for his children and his pride in them was the strongest force in his character, and this second blow drove him nearly out of his head. The girls hid from him in terror of their lives. Fury yielded to despair. He was at his wit's end. He was out of work, the children had no food. The landlord would wait no longer for the rent, and served him with a "dispossess notice." His boy was out of work, and in danger of arrest; his girl was disgraced, and his wife was anticipating the birth of a child.

Donovan did not like to borrow money, but on this occasion he determined to ask help from the church. Unfortunately both the Lady of Good

Cheer and the minister were away. He sought out the minister in charge, and requested a loan sufficient to cover the rent.

"He told me he had no money," said Donovan afterwards, "an' I see he was givin' it to me straight. He was broke as I was. He pulled out his watch and told me to put it up and take the cash, but I wouldn't stand fer the like o' that. A man that would do a minister out of his watch ought to light in a place five times hotter than they keep for gamblers and card cheats."

He went home undecided. His wife had just come in white and haggard from her work. She looked at him inquiringly, but spoke no word of complaint. Little Katie, who had heard he had gone out for food, was not so considerate. She ran up, her rosy cheeks streaked with grime where she had tried to rub away the tears of hunger.

"Dive Katie tum bread. Katie's hung'y," she said. There was not a morsel to eat in the house. Donovan looked around at the expectant hungry little faces, and saw as he glanced at his wife how she tried to hide her bleeding hands, and how bravely she was struggling to keep back the sobs. His eyes twitched, as he tried to blink away the tears. It was a topsy-turvy world, and a queer God to treat a man like this when all he wanted was to live straight and be a Christian. Then he shut his broken teeth together with a snap, and clenched his slender white hands.

" It's no use," he muttered to himself.

He got up without a word to his wife and went straight to the saloon to hunt up the friend of the poor, " the finest Christian gentleman in New York."

" Tom," he said, " lend me twenty-five dollars. I'll pay you back in a day or two."

" Sure, Jerry," said the great politician, " don't worry about it. I know you're on the square."

He went home and paid the rent and bought food for the children. That night he was back at the saloon. He picked up a game or two of cards, and soon had enough to pay off his debt to Hennessey.

Now there was plenty of food, and the house was once more well fitted up, as he redeemed all the articles he had put in pawn. His wife could stay at home and take care of her girls. She was no more the tired, fretful, worn-out toiler who drove her daughters into the street. The sweet spirit of motherhood shone again in her deep grey eyes and brooded over the house. The children were happy and well. All were well but Donovan. In his weak, shifty eyes, that used to twinkle with fun even on the darkest days, there was now a strange, dull weariness. A shadow had fallen upon him.

The Lady of Good Cheer found him thus on her return, and was cruelly hurt when she learned what had happened. She implored him to give up gambling, but he shook his head sadly and said: "What can I do? You know it's no use. I can't see the children starve."

She could not answer him, for she had sought the city from end to end in vain for work that he could do. With his weak eyes that shut him out from reading and writing, and his frail body, incapable of heavy toil, what was there he could do? She could not give up the hope that in some way the matter could be adjusted, and to-day they had been having a long talk over the possibilities before him. They were interrupted by the abrupt entrance of a woman, a strange looking creature, ragged and dishevelled, hard-featured and brazen-faced, with swollen features and coarse lines about her lips. She was unspeakably dirty, and in that neat pretty little home she looked decidedly out of place. She picked up a torn dirty shawl. "I come back fer me shawl," she said, and went out without further ado.

"Who is that woman?" asked the Lady of Good Cheer.

"When I was coming home from the saloon last night, I found her lying in the street, drunk," said Donovan. "I couldn't leave her there. That's no place fer a senseless woman to be lyin', with them toughs and hoboes hangin' around. She may not be any too good, but that's no reason why I should leave her to them fellers. So I got her up here, and she slept here all night."

Photo by J. H. Denison.

HOMELESS

"Where did she sleep? You haven't much extra room."

"She slept in my bed and I slept on the floor in here," said Donovan simply.

"But she's terribly dirty," said the Lady of Good Cheer.

"She is that," he answered. "It'll take my wife a day or two to clean out all she's left behind her. But what could I do? I ain't a good man. I can't be a Christian like you folks up at the church, but I can't have a poor woman lyin' on the street. Suppose it was my own daughter, now?"

Not many days after there was a knock at Donovan's door. At his invitation there entered a young gentleman arrayed in frock coat and silk hat, with patent leather shoes and lavender gloves, a most amazingly elegant figure for the fourth ward. Donovan looked him over with his shifting eyes for a minute or two in sheer astonishment, his head cocked on one side in his usual attitude of attention. Then suddenly he recognised him.

"Harkins!" he cried.

"Sure, it's me!" said the gorgeous personage, with a strained smile that betrayed some consciousness of his magnificence. "Didn't ye know me?"

Donovan rose from his seat and advanced toward him, his eyes twitching more and more rapidly, more than ever like a little bantam, as he looked up at the great six footer.

"You get out of here!" he said, biting off his

words angrily. "Do you hear me? You get out of here!"

Harkins' jaw dropped. He looked down at the little man in consternation.

"Why, Jerry!" he cried. "What's the matter? I thought you'd be glad to see me!"

"Matter!" cried Donovan. "You're an ingrate! That's what's the matter!"

"What do you mean?" asked Harkins.

"Well," said Donovan, "I found you when you was on the outs, in a saloon, when you didn't have a cent, or a friend to loan you one, or a bit to eat, and I took you into my house when I didn't have any too much myself, and I fed and took care of you. Ain't that so?"

"Sure it is," said Harkins.

"Well, you went away and got a good job, and you come back here when I was a drinkin', and there was nothin' to eat in the house. You had plenty of money in your pocket then, didn't you?"

"I was doing pretty well," admitted Harkins sheepishly.

"Well, you come in and saw Mrs. Donovan, and she told you how she was fixed, an' ye could see it yerself with half an eye. Did you come up and say, 'Mrs. Donovan, you was good to me when I was on the outs, and now I want to leave a fiver with you to help out a bit'? Not much you didn't! You turns on your heel, and leaves her and the children to starve! That's what I call an ingrate! And above all things on God's earth I hate an ingrate! Get out of my house!"

And the little man started forward so menacingly, that the six feet of gorgeous array in front of him slunk out of the door, and disappeared swiftly down the stairs.

V

FIVE years later Jerry Donovan and his friend Danny Riley boarded the Fall River boat one evening, on their way to Boston to visit an old friend. Danny Riley had been sexton of the church for many years, and had proved such a faithful assistant that the City Mission had finally engaged him to work among the men in the lodging-homes. He was stockily built, and had the swinging hitch in his walk that is characteristic of the old time Bowery boy. He had a broad, humorous Celtic face, and his wide mouth had a tendency to creep towards his ears in a comprehensive grin, whose expansive geniality was somewhat limited by a harsh upper lip which he had recently revealed by shaving his sandy moustache. His keen blue eyes could twinkle or flash as occasion demanded with the keenness of youth, though his crop of sandy hair was beginning to recede from its borders, and to show a few bare patches here and there.

They sat down in the cabin and watched the motley crowd pour in, rich and poor, gay and sad, some gaudy, some rusty. At first the two men from Chatham Square felt somewhat uncomfortable and out of place in this crowd of personages from up town. But their keen eyes soon noted the uncertain steps and eccentric behaviour of some of the gentlemen who passed, and their ears detected in the boisterous tones which they overheard some indications that the world above Fourteenth Street, which superficially was so far removed from the Bowery, was yet in its inmost nature subject to the same laws, controlled by the same forces, and in need of the same help.

" Say, half this gang is a bit leary eyed," said Danny, " and that woman with the bathtub hat give me the eye like one o' them Allen Street girls. This gang is as tough as any we've struck down in Doyers Street for sure."

" Why don't you hold a meeting, like the ones you ran there in Chinatown," said Jerry. " I'll help with the singing, and I'll tell 'em you're on the level, and I know it, though I ain't a Christian myself."

" I'm in for it if you are," said Dan. " We'll have to ask the captain fer a permit, or they'll put the cop on us."

So they rose and walked along the deck till they met a tall man resplendent in blue coat and gold braid.

" Say, Cap, kin we hold a gospel meeting on your boat to-night? " said Dan.

The captain looked in amazement at Dan with his Bowery walk, his shorn lip and bullet-head, and at the diminutive Jerry who stood surveying him out of the corners of his twitching eyes, while an apologetic smile parted his lips, and revealed his uneven teeth.

"We never have meetings on this boat," said the captain. "The people don't like to be bothered with them."

"Give us a show, Cap," said Dan. "You can come yourself, and if there's any kickin' you can shut us up."

"But who are you? How do I know you can hold a meeting?" asked the captain.

"I'm Lodging House Missionary of the City Mission," said Dan, pulling out his testimonials. "Try it on, Cap, and if the crowd don't like us and cry for more, you can tell us to chuck it any minute."

"All right," said the captain. "Go ahead. But mind if there's any complaint, you've got to stop."

"That's a go," said Dan. "Now, Jerry, get to work at the piano, and we'll give 'em a song or two."

Jerry sat down and hammered out a plaintive accompaniment, and they started in on "Where is My Wandering Boy To-night," Jerry making casual excursions into the tenor whenever the air seemed safe in Dan's hands. A crowd soon gathered, attracted by this unusual performance, and Dan said, "Now let's sing something every one knows." They tried "Throw Out the Life Line," and "Nearer My God to Thee," and under the stimulus of Dan's genial flattery, the crowd to its great amazement soon found itself singing lustily.

Dan read a few verses from the story of the Prodigal Son, and started in to speak: "I suppose you folks is wonderin' what two guys like us is up to, holdin' a meetin' on this here boat, so I may as well tell ye that I'm here to testify to the power of God to save and keep a man from the sin of drink. Thirteen years ago there wan't a hobo on the Bowery worse off than me. I was separated from my wife and child, because of the drink. I was good for nothin' but to hang around No. 9 Bowery or Barney's, wid me belly to the bar. You could float a good sized ship with the whisky I've drunk in my time. I was as bad a crook as any of 'em. There's no crime on the books I ain't been guilty of but murder. Me and the other 'bos hung around Chatham Square waitin' fer some gazabo ter come along that was fool enough fer us to handle him with the knockout drops or the black-jack, and we'd go through his clothes, and blow all we got on drink. Sometimes I'd go down to the Battery and hire meself out as a greenhorn to some rube from up the State, and off I'd go wid him, and wait fer a chance ter do him dirty, and back I'd come to blow in me cash in Chatham Square.

"Well, one day I'd just got out from doin' time fer a house-breakin' deal, and I was on me uppers fer fair. I'd blown in all the cash I had on the drink, and I'd even sold me clothes and was goin' about in relievers, the dirtiest, raggedest outfit ye ever see. I met a jigger comin' along down the Bowery, and I struck him fer some food. 'I'm starvin',' says I. 'I ain't had nothin' to eat for two days.' He looks me over kind o' sharp like, and then he says, 'Come in here, and I'll get you some dinner,' and he took me into Beef Steak John's and sat me down at the table and ordered a fine dinner. Well, I sat and looked at it. I couldn't eat so much as a mouthful. You boys know well enough when a man's on a spree he don't want no food. No more did I. All I wanted was the money to get a rosiner. So at last I had to own up to it. 'I can't eat,' says I. Well, he didn't get red-headed. He give me a little talk like a friend and then shook me hand, and give me a quarter. 'Friend,' says he, 'come and see me to-morrow at twelve at the church, and with God's help we'll make a man of you yet.' Well, friends, it was that hand-shake as saved me life. I went to see him the next day, thinking I could get more money out of him, but he give me such a talk, that before he got through I got right down on me knees and made a little prayer. Well, friends, that was thirteen years ago, and from that day to this, I ain't touched a drop of the stuff. They got me a job tendin' furnace, and a poor job it was, but I stuck to it, and then they got me a place in McClure's woodyard. And after some months I got me wife and little boy back again, and they made me sexton at the old Presbyterian Church. I ain't perfect, and I have me faults, but there ain't a man can point the fingers at me and say, 'Danny, you're fakin'.' They all know I'm on the level, and they know it's straight goods when I testify to the power of God to save and keep a man from the drink for thirteen years, eight months and ten days."

As he finished, Jerry sprang up. "That's straight, what he's tellin' ye," he said. "I've known Danny Riley fer eight years, and he's never touched a drop of the stuff. He's on the level, and you can bank on all he says. I ain't a Christian myself," he went on. "I wish to God I was. I tried to be, but it wasn't no use. I'm a professional card cheat, and I work in a poolroom on the Bowery. I wish to God I could get out of it. The only happy days of me life was when I was tryin' to be a Christian. I was hungry and sick, but I was all right in me mind, and I could say me prayers and go to church. Now when I hear them old songs, it makes me feel like cryin', fer I know I'm crooked. But I tell you, listen to what Danny says and you'll be all right. There ain't no other kind o' life worth livin' than what he's tellin' ye, an' ye can't be happy no other way. Only ye've got to be the real thing, on the level and no fakin'!"

Danny rose again. "Now if any of you people has been lettin' the devil run the show fer ye, or if the drink's been makin' a fool o' ye, cut it out! Start in, right away! to-night! I'm here to tell you that if ye get down on yer knees and say, 'God help me to cut out the booze!' if you mean business and no fakin', he'll surely help you and save you, like he did me. Only you've got to mean business."

Several men who had been drinking heavily stopped to talk with Danny, and Jerry sat by and watched with eager attention, his head tilted on one side, his eyes moving nervously in his excitement, while his friend was drawing from the penitents a promise to amend their lives. He tried to smile encouragingly at Danny, but his lips trembled, and now and then he furtively drew the back of his hand across his half blind eyes. "I wish to God I could be a good man," he muttered, "but it's no use."

THE END

www.ingramcontent.com/pod-product-compliance
Lightning Source LLC
LaVergne TN
LVHW020618110826
845149LV00002B/510

* 9 7 8 1 4 1 8 1 8 7 9 0 3 *